THE BONFIRE OF BERLIN

Helga Schneider was born in Steinberg (now in Poland, then in Germany) but spent her childhood in Berlin, where she was raised by her stepmother after being abandoned by her mother. She has lived in Bologna, Italy, since 1963, and is the author of *Let Me Go*.

ALSO BY HELGA SCHNEIDER

Let Me Go

Helga Schneider

THE BONFIRE OF BERLIN

TRANSLATED FROM THE ITALIAN BY
Shaun Whiteside

Published by Vintage 2006

4 6 8 10 9 7 5 3

Translated from the Italian, *Il rogo di Berlino*

First published in Great Britain in 2005 by
William Heinemann

Vintage
Random House, 20 Vauxhall Bridge Road,
London SW1V 2SA

Random House Australia (Pty) Limited
20 Alfred Street, Milsons Point, Sydney
New South Wales 2061, Australia

Random House New Zealand Limited
18 Poland Road, Glenfield,
Auckland 10, New Zealand

Random House (Pty) Limited
Isle of Houghton, Corner of Boundary Road & Carse O'Gowrie
Houghton 2198, South Africa

The Random House Group Limited Reg. No. 954009
www.randomhouse.co.uk/vintage

A CIP catalogue record for this book
is available from the British Library

ISBN 9780099443735 (from Jan 2007)
ISBN 0099443732

Papers used by Random House are natural, recyclable
products made from wood grown in sustainable forests.
The manufacturing processes conform to the environ-
mental regulations of the country of origin

Printed and bound in Great Britain by
Bookmarque Ltd, Croydon, Surrey

'Adolf Hitler is nothing but a vain bohemian from the streets. That people should be afraid of him is something that is really beyond my understanding.'

President Hindenburg on the occasion of a meeting between General Schleicher and the Bishop of Münster, 4 February 1931

Vienna, spring 1971

We hurried up the stairs of the old Viennese building, my heart thumping so hard that I couldn't ring the bell. Renzo, my son, rang it for me.

I had been looking for her for a long time. Now, thirty years after she had abandoned me in a Berlin already traumatised by war, I had found my mother again; she was back in Vienna, her home-town.

As for myself, I'd been born in Poland, I'd lived in Nazi Germany and been repatriated to Austria (also the country where my father had been born), and now I was settled in Italy; I had a husband and a son.

When the door opened, I saw a woman who looked strikingly like me. I gave her a tearful hug, over-whelmed by happiness and disbelief, and ready to understand, to forgive, to let bygones be bygones.

She immediately started talking, talking about herself. There was no attempt to justify her abandoning of me, no explanation of any kind.

She told me her story. Many years previously, she had been arrested in Birkenau concentration camp, where she had been a warder. She had been wearing an impeccable uniform 'that suited her terribly well'. Before twenty minutes had passed, she was opening a horrible wardrobe to show me, nostalgically, that very uniform. 'Why don't you try it on? I'd like to see it on you.' I didn't try it on; I was confused and upset. But what she then said was even worse, a denial of her role as a mother: 'I was condemned by the Nuremberg Court to six years' imprisonment as a war criminal, but none of that matters anymore. With Nazism I was somebody. Afterwards I was nothing.'

My blood froze. If she, in 1941, had decided that she didn't want her daughter, it was my turn not to want my mother! My son and I took the first train back to Italy. Renzo wept with disappointment. How could I explain why I hadn't found a mother, and he hadn't found a grandmother? He was only five years old.

So I lost my mother for the second time.

I don't know if she's still alive. Every now and again people ask me whether I've forgiven her.

I

Berlin, autumn 1941

My mother was a blonde woman who shouted *'Sieg Heil'* whenever Adolf Hitler appeared at rallies. Sometimes she brought me along, and one day I got lost in the crowd, finding myself alone when the square had emptied. My grandmother told me the story often, her words heavy with the hatred she felt for her daughter-in-law.

When my brother, Peter, was born, my mother discovered she had chosen the wrong career. Having convinced herself that serving the Führer's cause was more honourable than raising her own children, she abandoned us in a flat in Berlin-Niederschönhausen and enlisted in the SS. It was the autumn of 1941; the German forces were suffering badly on the Russian front.

We were taken in by Aunt Margarete, my father's sister. My father had left for the front some time before. Aunt Margarete lived in a villa in Berlin-Tempelhof, had a daughter, Eva, and was married to a count who was off fighting in the war as well.

At my aunt's villa, food rationing was unknown;

the table was always groaning with *foie gras*, canapés, various kinds of sausage, apple juice and fresh bread. I often stuffed myself until I could eat no more, only to throw it all up again, to my aunt's great consternation. I was four years old, my brother, Peter, nineteen months.

One day Aunt Margarete sent two cablegrams: one to my father, informing him of his wife's desertion, news that gave him an attack of jaundice; the other to our paternal grandmother, who immediately put my father's elder sister in charge of her already impoverished farm and rushed from troubled Poland to equally troubled Berlin.

My grandmother arrived smelling of poultry and aniseed biscuits, deposited her suitcase and her umbrella by the empty swimming pool, cast a withering glance at the liveried butler with his Hitler moustache who was fawning on my aunt with ludicrous zeal, and started swearing like a trooper. Calling my mother a *Nazihure*, a Nazi whore, she considered our fate. She had clear ideas about what should happen to us.

Aunt Margarete was willing to bring up Peter and me along with Eva, but my grandmother was having none of it. Worried that her daughter would turn us into two little manikins, she insisted on taking us to Poland. The two women had a heated conversation beside the pool. Soon another cablegram made its way to the front, but it was my father's view that we should stay in Berlin. So our grandmother settled with Peter and me in the Niederschönhausen flat to await developments. She eradicated all traces of my mother, as though the house had been infested with plague.

6

However, she found a way to renew her memory every day by talking about her in unrepeatable terms, adding fresh hatred to old rancour.

Grandmother was both loving and severe. She punished me without hesitation whenever I told lies, and I told them often. I liked to go around saying, for example, that my father was a famous General, while in reality he was only a soldier in an anti-aircraft division, and furthermore he was a fervent anti-militarist. An Army career had always been the least of his ambitions. His presence in Berlin had a great deal to do with the fact that his sister Margarete lived there; being so well connected, it seemed likely that she would be able to able to open a few doors for him. He had found himself involved in the war in spite of himself, due to the German annexation of Austria. Having been born in Vienna, he was irritated at having to wear the uniform of the *Wehrmacht*, though such sentiments were not openly expressed in those days.

My lie about my father the General was the product of a need to overcompensate. I had been deprived of maternal warmth, and although I loved my grandmother very much, I had focused my entire being on my father. But as he was far away, it was essential for me to create a fantasy substitute for myself. That is why I devised the legend of my father the General, a fantasy that gave me great consolation, particularly when other people expressed their admiration for this 'hero of the Fatherland'! Who could command greater respect than a brave General fighting to save the German people from Bolshevism?

*

7

In Niederschönhausen there was a cobbled yard called the Böllerhof. Our grandmother took us there to play. All the children loved her for her cheerfulness. She had a vivid imagination and a rather girlish manner. She was always making up new games, allowing us to forget the war for a while. She would sing in Polish, and we would listen with delight even if we didn't understand a word. In that bare yard she sang and danced, moving with grace, with an innocent, traditional spontaneity; everyone loved her, and I was sometimes jealous of her. But often, in the middle of her performances, the sirens would scream, and we would have to run to the shelter in the cellar. The spell would be broken.

Grandmother was fat and poetic, and blessed with a keen intelligence. She listened to the BBC in secret and told us about the course the war was taking, although Peter and I didn't understand what she was talking about. We knew only that war meant hunger, sirens, fear and bombs. To help us go to sleep, Grandmother told us fairy-tales from the Black Forest in a mixture of German and Polish. Her voice gave us the reassurance we so badly needed.

Early in the summer of 1942, my father came to Berlin on leave, and Aunt Margarete gave a little party in his honour. The guests included a beautiful young woman called Ursula. At the party Peter and I ate our fill of canapés. Peter threw up twice; I got hiccups. My cousin Eva looked at us as though we were two Cinderellas she was ashamed of. Eva's vanity made me feel inferior, and I was happy that we hadn't ended up living with her.

That evening, between one mouthful and the next, I noticed that my father was spending a lot of time with Ursula. She was flirting with him, and he was flirting back! I felt embarrassed and curious at the same time. What was going on?

The only thing that cheered me up when the party came to an end was the hope that my father would never see Ursula again.

During the days that followed, I managed to spend some time with him, but something was wrong. I found him reserved and distant, and began to feel uneasy. He only had three days' leave; then he returned to the front.

I was confused.

My father, slim and handsome, with his high forehead and wavy hair, his thoughtful artist's expression as he absorbed colours, sounds and emotions – my father, with his considered gestures, his low, seductive voice – had nothing at all to do with the heroic General of my imagination, so it was difficult for me to reconcile him with my ideal.

Meanwhile the war had been growing more and more intense; as air-raids became more frequent, food supplies dwindled. Grandmother often returned from the shops empty-handed, and when that happened all we had for dinner was a glass of water. To make us forget our hunger, she would tell us fairy-tales or sing us Polish peasant songs.

One morning she began cursing loudly and broke a beautiful gilded coffee-pot. Hurling it to the kitchen floor, she shouted, 'What an idiot! What a fool!' My father had written to tell her that he had got engaged to Ursula. After their meeting at Aunt Margarete's villa, they had corresponded, and now they had decided to marry. My grandmother was beside herself. 'For heaven's sake!' she yelled. 'Just a year ago your father was devastated when that good-for-nothing mother of yours abandoned him, and now he's getting ready to marry again! What an idiot! What a fool!'

She couldn't get used to the idea. She said that Ursula was too young to take on two children who were not her own, and where she had previously spoken of my mother in the most appalling terms, she now lambasted my father for having sought conso-lation so quickly. All her indignation counted for nothing. The two love-birds had already set a date for their wedding.

When Grandmother realised there was nothing to be done, she packed her suitcase, grabbed my grand-father's umbrella like a bayonet and set off for Poland, swearing that she never wanted to see her son again, let alone his new bride. Poor Grandmother, she had so looked forward to raising us.

Once Grandmother had gone, I felt lost. She had given us love and joy and, in spite of the war, a sense of security. I was inconsolable and hated Aunt Margarete for bringing my father and Ursula together. We were parked once more at the Tempelhof villa to allow the newlyweds to spend a brief honeymoon in Ursula's rented flat in Friedrichsruher Strasse in Berlin-Steglitz. I tried to suppress the pain of separation from my grandmother by filling myself up with food. I ate and threw up while Eva looked on in disgust.

*

It was September. Life at the villa continued as usual. The deaf-mute gardener went on pruning the hedges, and the war seemed only to concern people unfortunate enough to live beyond the big gate capped by the family crest.

Eva was unbearable. Possessive of her dolls, she would not let me touch them under any circumstances. Apart from that, she affected such exaggerated aristocratic manners that I laughed until I was fit to burst.

Aunt Margarete was tall, slim, austere and very beautiful. She had magnificent red hair and splendid skin, white and transparent, with a scattering of pale freckles. She was extremely elegant and wore hats with little veils. When she kissed us goodnight, I could smell a faint perfume that lingered in the room until morning. Three years later, sad to say, she would kill herself with Veronal. I never knew why. My grandmother was given to understand that her daughter had died of pneumonia.

Peter was a terrible child and kept everyone on edge. On two occasions he threatened to throw himself into the empty swimming-pool, and on another he swallowed a little chocolate made of porcelain which gave him a terrible stomach-ache. Not a day went by when he wasn't up to some mischief or other.

After this short honeymoon, my father returned to the front, and we went to live with our stepmother in Friedrichsruher Strasse. I was troubled and anxious. The war was worsening rapidly. Air-raids were becoming more frequent and intense, and Ursula complained of the lack of safety in our cellar. On top of that, it was becoming increasingly difficult to find provisions: rationing was not working, and all the shops were empty. You couldn't find as much as a ball of thread. Old people were dying because of the growing scarcity of food and medicines, particularly those for serious illnesses.

At first Aunt Margarete would send her chauffeur over with a food parcel every now and again, but soon she stopped doing that: even at the villa, things weren't going as well as they had been. Ursula maintained her youthful and carefree appearance despite the fact that she was growing thinner before our eyes. She had beautiful ash-blonde hair and eyes bluer than Peter's! My brother would sniff her shoes or kiss her on the chin, and she would laugh and pinch his bottom. In the wink of an eye he had begun to call her Mutti, something I was incapable of doing. The word stuck in my throat. I could say Wutti, or Lutti, or Butti, but Mutti was impossible. This was the first in a long series of difficulties.

I soon came to realise that Ursula employed a double standard when dealing with Peter and with me. Whenever he did something wrong, she found an excuse, as often as not his tender age. When I did something wrong, she would declare that I was my mother's daughter. She criticised Grandmother's way of raising us, saying it was too permissive. I didn't agree; Grandmother had been anything but per-missive. Maternal and fair but never weak.

Some of Ursula's attitudes alarmed me. If I did

something wrong, I would stammer, 'But I thought . . .'; she would interrupt me, shouting, 'You're not supposed to think, you're supposed to obey!' My blood would go cold. Obeying without thinking: I couldn't accept such an order from anyone!

She couldn't bear to be contradicted, either. And when I stood my ground, she punished me. Blind German submission was an absolute for her.

Her chosen place of punishment was the study where my father kept his things: his books, his typewriter, his canvases and his paints. In time I came to hate that studio, filled though it was with traces of him. Apart from being locked in that room, I was given other punishments as well, some of which were truly oppressive. For example, Ursula demanded that I pick out the fluff from the precious Persian carpet she had brought as part of her dowry; she made me stay on my hands and knees until even the tiniest hair was gone. Sometimes I had to continue until the dust gave me a coughing fit.

Another thing Ursula wouldn't put up with was my innocent lie about my father the General. One day she caught me repeating it to Frau Gerlinde, a friend of hers who lived on the same floor and who sometimes dropped in for a chat. My stepmother had gone to fetch Frau Gerlinde a glass of water, and as she came back into the room she caught me telling my fairytale. She interrupted me roughly, shouting, 'That fib again! You really are incorrigible! You're just like your mother, a fake and a liar!' Then she announced in an authoritarian voice, 'Your-father-is-in-the-anti-aircraft-division, say "anti-aircraft" after me, foolish girl!'

'It's not true!' I cried, shaking with humiliation. 'My father is a famous General!'

'He's in the anti-aircraft division, I tell you!' she shrieked, red with fury.

'He's a General!'

Then she started to slap me in front of Frau Gerlinde, repeating that I was just like my mother. Finally she sent me to the study with the peremptory declaration 'No dinner for you tonight!'

There was one other thing she couldn't bear; the fact that, at the age of five, I was still sucking my thumb. She tried everything she could think of to break my habit: sprinkling my finger with salt, then with perfume, then with turpentine, half a bottle of which she had found in my father's studio. Having run out of unpleasant concoctions, she took to striking my thumb with a variety of objects: wooden spoons, a letter-opener, the handle of the carpet-beater.

One day she struck me so violently that I almost fainted from the pain, but instead I bit her on the wrist and fled to the bathroom and locked myself in. She started knocking furiously at the door, threatening me with a variety of punishments if I didn't open up straight away, but I refused to do so, fearing that she might kill me. Crouching under the window, I waited to see what would happen.

Ursula went on knocking and threatening but in the end was obliged to call someone to force the door. I heard a lot of fussing around the lock until it gave and my stepmother burst in like a Fury. She grabbed me by the hair and hit me in front of the person who had helped her to open the door, a bent and emaciated old man with a bald head who gave me an awkward smile of solidarity.

When the old man had gone, Ursula dispatched me to the study as usual, with a series of kicks to the bottom, denying me, as she always did, my food ration. Towards evening, by now crazed with hunger, I became enraged. I started to search for something on which I could vent my rage. Finally my eye fell on some little tubes of paint lined up on a small wicker table; at the same time I noticed a canvas on an easel. It showed an interior with a bowl full of apples, pears, grapes and other fruits with which I was unfamiliar.

I picked up a tube, unscrewed the cap and, with my fingers, smeared the entire contents over the canvas, obliterating pears, apples, grapes and exotic fruits and reducing the whole thing to formless, dark brown mud. When my stepmother saw the destruction, she nearly strangled me. She broke a coat-hanger over my bare bottom and shouted, 'What else could anyone expect of the daughter of a Nazi whore?'

She shouldn't have said that! From that day onwards, our relationship became one of open hostility. I began to think about how I could avenge myself.

One morning Ursula went out shopping: someone had said there was more to buy than usual, including potatoes and molasses. She left Peter and me in the care of Frau Gerlinde.

Frau Gerlinde was a young woman, sweet and kind,

whose husband was also at the front; they had no children.

She sat down on the sofa in the drawing room and started to read us a fairy-tale; Peter listened wide-eyed. But in the middle of a scene between the wicked witch and some innocent creature or other, I announced that I had to go to the bathroom. Frau Gerlinde nodded and smiled, though Peter was furious with me for ruining the suspense. I left the room, but rather than going to the bathroom I slipped into Ursula's bedroom and started rummaging in the chest of drawers. I found something very interesting.

It was a pile of letters tied with a red ribbon; I guessed immediately that these were letters my father had written to Ursula from the front. Hiding the packet in my knickers, I slipped into the bathroom. I had to act quickly because my stepmother had taken to hiding the key after I'd locked myself in. I quickly tore the letters to bits, threw the pieces into the toilet-bowl and pulled the chain. I got back to the drawing room just in time to enjoy the end of the fairy-tale.

My stepmother discovered the crime a few days later and didn't think for as much as a moment that it might have been Peter. She beat me mercilessly with another coat-hanger, which, as usual, broke in two. Then she sent me to my father's study, where she tied my arms to a chair. I stayed there all day in the dark, without anything to eat. When, towards evening, she finally untied me, I fainted at her feet.

When I came to my senses, I was lying on the sofa in the drawing room. Ursula was looking at me in silence. Her young face was irritated, almost threatening. I saw it in the faint halo of light coming from a standard lamp; her eyes were cold.

'How do you feel?' she asked finally, without a hint of tenderness.

'Fine,' I murmured. The memory emerged slowly: my father's study, the darkness, the chair, the ropes.

'Can you get up?'

I jumped from the sofa so quickly that my eyes clouded over. I swayed back and forth.

'Gently, young lady,' she said. 'You're laying it on as you always do!' And she pushed me into a chair. 'I'll be back in a minute,' she added, and left the room. I remained with Peter, who pressed me with questions. 'Why did you fall? Why did Mutti carry you to the sofa! Why has Mutti gone out! Why don't you get up?'

My stepmother returned with a cup of something that was supposed to be milk but was really just a plastery broth made from a strange powder and not even sweetened.

'Drink!'

I shook my head.

'Drink!' she repeated impatiently. So I gulped down the disgusting potion with Peter aping my grimaces.

After a while, my stepmother announced, 'I have something to say to you, Helga.'

I looked at her, trying to guess what she was about to tell me.

'We can't go on like this,' she began. 'I'm not going to put up with it any longer. You're forcing me to send you away to boarding school.'

Peter piped up, 'Me too bo'ding school! Me too!'

'You're staying with Mutti,' Ursula hushed him. 'You're a good boy.' At which, flattered, he half-closed his eyes.

My stepmother stared at me and waited for my reply, which didn't come. 'Don't you have anything to say?' she asked, rather startled.

'No.'

'Then you don't mind if I send you to boarding school?' she persisted, unsettled by my indifference.

'No.'

A perplexed expression flickered across her face. 'Do you understand what I'm telling you?'

I nodded.

'I've decided to send you to boarding school! Because you're rebellious, stubborn and . . .' But the rest of her words were drowned out by sirens. 'Not again!' she exclaimed. We ran to the cellar.

The general situation was getting worse. We were always hungry and frequently went to bed without supper. Rationing didn't cover even the most basic requirements. But in spite of the fact that we were seriously malnourished, Peter kept his round cherub's face. He was a truly beautiful child: blond curls, delicate features, big blue eyes; who could have resisted him? As for me, God had seen fit to give me hair straight as wires and eyes that were no match for Peter's.

One morning Ursula dealt me another severe blow. In the street we had met some of her friends who worked for a military hospital, and she had calmly introduced Peter as her son and me as her step-daughter. That convinced me once and for all that she had accepted him and not me. I was a mere appendage, and an ungrateful one at that. I felt alone and unwanted, and only wished to die.

One afternoon – we had just got back from the shelter after a severe air-raid – my stepmother went to ask Frau Gerlinde if she could borrow something. Seized by a sudden impulse, I crept through our front door, went down the stairs and slipped into the courtyard. This was one of those typical Berlin court-yards you find inside big blocks of flats, dense with vegetation.

I wandered about the little asphalt paths, trying to keep out of sight. In the end I stopped where the women usually went to beat their carpets, but there was not a soul to be seen. The sparrows were hopping about in the sunbeams and rose into the air with an indignant commotion. I swung from a beam with my legs in the air and my head dangling, and watched the world upside down; soon my head was spinning.

The place was quiet, surrounded by tall trees, and the canopy of branches and leaves concealed the sky. A strong smell of autumn and mould hung in the air.

I became aware of how isolated I was, and all of a sudden a profound loneliness swept through me with such violence that it left me feeling stunned and anxious.

I started crying, sobbing loudly and dejectedly. I wept for a long time, and the harder I wept the angrier and more rebellious I felt: God couldn't hear me! He would not stop punishing me. First he had taken away my father, then my mother, finally my grandmother too. Why did I have to stay with my stepmother? She didn't love me! I started to kick a tree trunk, but in fact I was kicking God. 'If you exist,' I thought furiously, 'give me a sign!' As I was kicking the tree in a blind fury, I saw a cat emerge from beneath a bush. It was grey with white stripes, and had yellow eyes. It stared at me intently. Finally it came over and rubbed against my legs with gentle familiarity. That contact, that gesture of solidarity, made me start sobbing again but this time with gratitude. I convinced myself that God was trying to reassure me.

After some time I heard Ursula calling me from the kitchen window. Although she couldn't see me, I drew back to hide behind the fat trunk of a tree. 'Heeeelgaaaaa!' she shouted.

I didn't reply. No, I didn't want to go back to her, I never wanted to go back to that house. Then I went and hid behind a bush whose spiny branches scratched my arms and face. I felt one of my eyebrows tearing, and blood ran down my face to the corner of my mouth. I wiped it away with a handful of dry leaves. The cat had vanished.

All of a sudden the wind came up, shaking the branches of the trees, unleashing a whirl of dead leaves. The leaves fell drunkenly, like big, lost butterflies joining their fellows in death.

Once again I heard my stepmother's voice, closer this time. She must have come down to the courtyard. She persisted: 'Helgaaa! Helgaaa!' In her voice there was a mixture of irritation and concern, as though she was obliged by circumstance to worry about something that did not really touch her heart. Other voices joined hers, and I realised that she had roused the neighbours. I became frightened. I hid myself even further inside the bush, still dabbing at my cut eyebrow. The voices were getting closer. All of a sudden I heard my stepmother right in front of me: 'She's gone too far this time, I'm not having it any more! She's an impossible child, she's making me crazy!' The voices went on calling me, each with a different intonation; I didn't budge. After a while they moved off, and all that remained was the wind.

I started breathing again. Night was falling quickly. It was as though someone had stretched a dark cloth over a lampshade, then added others in quick succession. I was cold and hungry, but I didn't want to go back to my stepmother for anything.

Soon, beyond the roofs, I heard a dark rumble, like the sound of planes; as the sirens hadn't sounded, I hoped it was only a thunderstorm. A big drop of rain fell on my forehead, so I decided to take shelter. There were no voices now, no footsteps. The tree-trunks and bushes were dark, sinister shadows; I imagined I was surrounded by goblins that were spying on me; perhaps they were benevolent, perhaps merely curious.

In the end I extricated myself from the bush and made it back to the main path. I ran towards the door into the entrance hall and caught my breath.

Everything was dark and deserted. I pressed the light-switch, but the power was so feeble that I could hardly see a thing. What should I do?

I opened the door to the cellar, which had been left unlocked to allow access during air-raids. I ran my hand along the wall until I felt the hard knob of the switch, but the light that came on was merely a glimmer.

I smelled the damp cellar smell, then went down the concrete steps, a cold wind blowing against my neck.

A long corridor opened up at the foot of the stairs, leading in two directions; I hesitated. Usually, when the siren sounded, we would take the left turn to reach the room that served as a shelter; I decided to investigate what lay to the right.

I saw legless chairs and armless dolls, dusty trunks and a perfectly preserved tailor's dummy. The light was faint and flickering.

Finally I reached the gloomy bowels of the building, where the coal was stored. I saw a mountain of briquettes and a smaller one of coke. Two shovels and a broom leaned against the wall. On a rudimentary shelf there was a pile of jute sacks.

With cold determination, I decided to avenge myself on Ursula. I would stay out all night, I would make her die of worry.

Between the pile of coal and the wall, I discovered an empty space: just what I was looking for!

I went back to the shelf and took down all the sacks. With some of them I made a kind of bed, planning to cover myself with the rest.

I contemplated my work with a sudden sense of unease: what would happen to me once it was totally dark? But my desire for revenge was stronger than my fear. I gritted my teeth, lay down on my makeshift bed and waited for the light to go out.

All of a sudden darkness swooped upon me like a

great bat. I cried out and found that I was drenched in sweat.

The darkness was dense and menacing. I heard hisses, murmurs, the strangest noises. I began to imagine the creatures creeping around me – rats, spiders or millipedes – and was tempted to get up, switch on the light, go back to the flat and prostrate myself at Ursula's feet. But I resisted. I clenched my fists and wept with fear.

All of a sudden I heard the creak of the cellar door and footsteps scurrying down the steps. Muffled voices were calling to me: 'Helga! Where are you?'

I didn't move a muscle. All of a sudden someone came into the coal-cellar and turned on the light. There must have been four or five women, judging by the sounds their shoes made. One of them said: 'She isn't here either, wherever can the poor child be?' I heard my stepmother's voice: 'She'll pay for this, how she'll pay for this!' Then they left.

I heard the door closing. I was on my own again.

II

I awoke with a start: a chorus of voices was calling me from the path outside: 'Helga! Helga!'

I got up but suddenly felt terribly dizzy. I waited for my lightheadedness to pass, then shook off the sacks; I was literally covered in coal. My arms had been scratched to bits by the spines of the bush I'd hidden in, and I was faint with hunger.

A dim light shone through the air vents, faintly illuminating the coal pile. The place had lost its sinister atmosphere and was merely a cellar.

I hurried down the corridor to the steps, opened the door quietly and, seeing no-one, slipped into the entrance hall.

But it was cold there, so I ran into the courtyard. The slanting light of early morning gave no warmth, but it did comfort me. The frost was melting on the paths.

As there had been no sirens that night, I knew that the enemy must have taken the day off.

I started wandering the paths, battling against terrible hunger pangs. A single long, grainy cloud stretched in the sky like a bank of pumice. I was almost drunk with weakness and would have eaten the bark off a tree.

In fact I very much wanted someone to find me, and, all of a sudden, a group of women emerged from nowhere and ran towards me. 'There you are! Thank heavens you're alive! What on earth happened to you!' One of them said to me, 'Your mother's been looking for you since yesterday.'

'She isn't my mother,' I replied darkly.

'Anyway, we're going to take you home,' the woman said resolutely, and at that moment my step-mother turned up, shouting, 'So there you are! Might we know where you've been hiding? The whole neighbourhood has been out looking for you. What point were you trying to make? None of us has slept a wink, do you realise? You come home right now, and we'll have a long talk!' She thanked the others and dragged me away, reprimanding me all the while. When we got to our flat, Hilde, Ursula's sister, was there too. I had only seen her twice since we'd been living in Friedrichsruher Strasse. She was six years older than my stepmother and worked at the Ministry of Propaganda. Peter gave me a frightened glance and hid behind a door. I must have looked truly terrible!

Ursula pushed me into a chair and, with Teutonic energy, began issuing orders: 'You're going to tell me every last thing! Where have you been? Where did you sleep last night? I nearly called the police! Speak, damn you!' There were two small red spots at the tops of her cheekbones.

'I'm hungry,' was the only thing I could manage to say. My stomach was gripped with cramps, paralysing my mind. 'I'm hungry too!' Peter cried out, reappearing from behind the door. But my stepmother dismissed him with unusual harshness: 'You've already eaten, little boy!' Peter screwed up his mouth and stared at her in disbelief.

'I think you should give her something to eat,' Hilde said firmly.

'Not a bit of it!' exclaimed my stepmother. 'First she must speak, the swine!' And she struck the table with her fist. But I couldn't think straight. I was so weak that I saw everything double: Peter had four eyes, Hilde two noses. Then Ursula yielded and gave me the usual dishwater that looked like milk and hadn't even been warmed up, adding a slice of damp bread so thin it was almost transparent.

I ate greedily while my stepmother complained to her sister: 'I've had it up to here, Hilde, I can tell you! This child will be the death of me!'

'Why don't you have her analysed?' Hilde asked, coldly pragmatic. 'I know a group of child psychologists. Why not consult them? It's not impossible that the child has problems, she might need treatment.'

'Perhaps you're right,' agreed my stepmother. 'Could you contact them for me?' Hilde promised she would.

And sure enough, a few days later, my stepmother led me to a building where we were taken to a big room with lots of windows looking out on to a cluster of fir trees. Two doctors, a man and a woman, asked me lots of questions, and asked me to do some drawings. I found it all rather amusing. Less amusing was what my stepmother said afterwards. She informed me that the psychologists had found me to be suffering from an 'illness' and that I would have to spend time in an institution, where I would be cured. I never found out what that illness might have been, but a few days later, Ursula packed a small suitcase with my things, left Peter with Frau Gerlinde, gave me a plate of semolina (that set off alarm bells) and announced, 'I'm taking you to the institution today.' I started crying, but she was not to be moved.

It was a foggy day, and I was tired. There had been an air-raid, and we had had to dash to the cellar, so we hadn't slept much. I was frightened and dejected. My stepmother was showing the power she had over me: she could get rid of me by sending me to an institution, and there was nothing I could do about it. We were crossing the little cobbled square in front of Steglitz station when all of a sudden the siren sounded. We ran for the nearest shelter, but at first the people wouldn't let us in. Then my stepmother started shouting, threatening to tell the Gestapo. They let us in then.

Once the raid was over, we got on a train, though it stopped for two false alarms.

In our compartment there was a group of Hitler Youth who, despite the heavy air-raid, were singing at the top of their voices: 'A flower blossoms on the moor, its name is Erika!' They were rumbustious and euphoric, and they radiated a barely imaginable joy.

We got off the train in a part of the city that had been seriously damaged by bombs and, after walking for fifteen minutes, arrived at a large black door set in a stone wall with barbed wire running along the top. A uniformed woman with a threatening expression snapped, 'Papers!', then let us into a foggy courtyard that echoed with the furious barking of a pack of guard dogs.

Through the fog we glimpsed a large, hostile-looking building; small windows were hidden behind black grilles, and no smoke issued from the chimney. Just like the building I had drawn a few days previously for the psychologists.

We stopped in front of a large door with spy-holes. A bell rang shrilly inside; someone behind the door stared at us for a long time. It started raining. Within moments we were drenched; my brown hood was as useless as a rag, and my stepmother's hair, which she had combed carefully, fell into her face like a crumbling pyramid. After a considerable wait we were allowed in.

Ursula asked for information from a woman holed up in a little cage like a captive owl. Two cold eyes scrutinised us. 'First floor!' the woman grunted finally. 'Second corridor on the right, room four! *Heil Hitler!*'

Our dripping hoods left enormous puddles on the parquet of the entrance hall as we began to climb the stairs. The steps were very smooth, and I slipped and hurt my shoulder quite badly. I cried out, the owl poked her head out of her little cage, and I was suddenly struck by a wave of nausea that was reinforced by a smell of cabbage like a toxic cloud. My step-mother sighed angrily: 'Why don't you watch where you put your feet?'

We found the room the owl had directed us to; some women were looking after a group of disabled children: a little blind girl, a little boy waving his arms around and dribbling, two retarded children and a little girl in a wheelchair. I didn't understand.

We waited for a long time in the freezing room. At last we were seen by a bony old woman with very white hair pulled back in a chignon. She carefully examined the sheets of paper handed to her by my stepmother and finally, after staring at me intensely through her pince-nez, observed, 'I don't think this is the right place for your daughter, madam.' Ursula was clearly annoyed. Her voice grew shrill as she explained that the eminent team of psychologists who had examined me had warmly recommended the institution. Then she lowered her voice and added something that I couldn't quite hear. The woman started consulting the pieces of paper again, pondered, polished away at her glasses for a long time and said, 'Fine, madam, I will make an exception and accept your child.'

My stepmother heaved a sigh of relief, for which I hated her. Quivering with gratitude, she went to grip the woman's hand, but the woman pulled it away abruptly, turned towards her desk, put a cold, dry hand on my head and said, 'Now it's time to say goodbye to your mother, Helga. It's getting late, and I have people waiting for me outside.' But I turned away from my stepmother so she wouldn't have the satisfaction of seeing my tears.

III

Berlin, 1942

The place turned out to be a kind of hell; everything there was unbearable.

It was, in fact, a storehouse for unwanted children, for those who were considered unworthy of belonging to the Aryan race because they were blind, deaf-mute, crippled, paralysed, dwarfs, subnormal and so on.

The first thing they did was to shear off my hair as a precaution against lice. Then they made me put on a uniform with black stripes, like the ones worn by convicts. The food was meagre and of poor quality, and the staff were overbearing and icily formal.

I endured various unpleasant medical examinations, including one by a gynaecologist. I was given pills which dulled my senses.

The rules were severe, and we were punished for the slightest misdemeanour by having our food withdrawn, being beaten or being left in a dark room. But most ludicrous of all was the so-called 'socialisation hour' to which we had to submit every day.

On these occasions, children with the most diverse pathologies were crammed together in a tiny space where they inevitably came into conflict with one another. When scuffles broke out, the one supervisor pretended not to see anything and failed to intervene. Survival of the fittest was the rule.

One day a blind boy, panicking in the insane hubbub, attached himself to my ear, biting it so furiously that I was afraid he was going to pull it off. The supervisor didn't bat an eyelid.

During socialisation hour I witnessed the most appalling scenes, and I gradually convinced myself that someone was spying on us through two-way mirrors. It was a horrible sensation.

On other occasions they would call us one by one into a chilly underground room to subject us to such intimate and embarrassing examinations that we almost felt we'd been raped. Our families were allowed to visit us once a month, but the rumour was that hardly anyone ever turned up. The worst time was when the sirens went. Indescribable chaos usually broke out. The building echoed with orders and confused shouts, everyone dashed towards the only staircase, shrieking, pushing and kicking until panic was inevitable. On these occasions I found myself covered with bruises.

The more time passed, the worse I felt. I had entered the institution in reasonably good health, but now I suffered illness after illness – fits of vomiting, apathy, weeping, asthma. On one occasion I was unable to breathe for almost a minute; the nurses helped me by hitting me hard on the back, slapping me and applying pressure to my thorax. Finally one of them gave me an injection with a blunt needle. I got my breath back, but blood came pouring out of my mouth. The following day I was tested for tuberculosis, but the test was negative.

One morning I discovered that I had wet the bed, and my torments began in earnest. I had hoped this was a unique event, but it soon happened again. I attracted the dislike of the orderlies, who always took a mischievous delight in reporting the misdeed to their superiors. I tried to conquer my weakness, but it only got worse. If at first I was wetting the bed two or three times a week, in the end it happened every night.

At first I was punished by having my meals suspended. When that proved useless, it was followed by a series of beatings. I was given a black eye and limped for a few days, but I still peed in my sleep. The orderlies called me 'piss-the-bed', a nickname that stuck like a stain. They decided to punish me with the 'dark room'.

This was an isolation cell in the basement. It was cold and bare, there was nothing but a camp bed and a chamber pot, and the walls were so thick that neither the barks of the dogs nor the screams of the sirens could penetrate them. The minimum stay was twelve hours, and in the most serious cases punishment could continue for as many as three or four days. And of course one was hardly given any food.

But not even the dark room could make me stop; I had entered a vicious circle. I wet the bed, I was sent to the dark room, and when they took me out I was so terrified that I wet it again.

I started to fear for my life and considered the possibility of escaping, but that proved to be impossible. The courtyard was full of ferocious dogs, and I wouldn't have escaped alive. What was I to do? Write to my grandmother? I doubted whether the letter would ever be sent. Call in my stepmother? That was out of the question; she was glad to be rid of me! So I resorted to the only weapon at my disposal: I stopped eating.

At first they tried to force-feed me, ramming food down my throat until my oesophagus was damaged. In the end they just left me in bed because I couldn't even stand. I passed my days in a torpor, in my few lucid moments thinking of my father and grandmother. One morning, however, I saw my stepmother standing by my bed.

Her eyes hard, she said, 'They called me in to bring you home, they've decided you're a hopeless case!' I didn't say a word, not least because I was so weak. 'Going on hunger strike,' my stepmother said contemptuously. 'What a wicked idea! It's clearer than it ever was that you're your mother's daughter!'

The prospect of going home cleared my head.

My stepmother paced back and forth in the empty dormitory, finally stopping by the window. For a moment she looked out at the courtyard, where the dogs were barking. They barked, day and night, at the slightest disturbance.

I looked at Ursula's back: it was narrow, with protruding shoulder-blades. Her hair was covered with a headscarf, and she looked small because she wasn't wearing her high heels. She looked older, too, and more exhausted. All of a sudden she turned round and said sharply, 'If you want to come with me, you're going to have to get off that bed.'

I was afraid I wouldn't be able to. For a number of days I had only got out of bed to use the chamber pot, and now the thought of having to get dressed and actually leave the building seemed beyond me. Nonetheless I forced myself. Sitting on the edge of the bed, I waited for my head to stop spinning. Thinking of my grandmother, I silently invoked her help.

Finally I found the strength to get to my feet, while my stepmother looked on impassively. I wondered why I deserved such harsh treatment. Then an orderly brought my things and dumped them on the bed, exchanging a glance with my stepmother. Ursula threw my few belongings into my little suitcase with impatient gestures. Perhaps I had spoiled her plans. I got dressed on my own, struggling against my weakness. Perhaps she hoped I wouldn't be able to do it, perhaps she hoped she would be forced to leave me in the institution, but the thought of escaping spurred me on and filled me with energy. Once the formalities were complete, we left the building. I realised that Ursula was ashamed of my shaven head. People were giving me curious stares on the *S-Bahn*.

When we got home, Peter welcomed me with a little shriek of horror, hiding behind the legs of his beloved Mutti.

I had been so traumatised by the institution that life with my stepmother seemed a paradise in comparison. I did everything I could to be accepted: I was polite and humble, I forced myself to obey without thinking, without talking back, but as before it was all to no avail; she didn't want me. Winter passed, but in the spring I had to go away again. This time it was to a re-education school for children with personality disorders. When Ursula told me about it, I fell into a state of despair. I wept and thought more than once of running away from home, but she never took her eye off the door, and she had trained Peter to act as my guard.

One day I saw my little suitcase packed once more and realised the time had come. We left very early in the morning. Through the loudspeakers in the *S-Bahn* station, Goebbels ranted about victory and liberation, while people standing in little groups listened in silence. Their faces were tense, weary and sceptical.

The school was in Oranienburg-Eden, on the far outskirts of Berlin. We boarded an already crowded train. In Oranienburg we were told that the bus that should have taken us to Eden was no longer running due to the petrol shortage, so we had to continue on foot. Walking along a dung-scattered main road lined with old trees, we met some horse-drawn carts. As I followed my stepmother, my heart was anxious. What would the school be like? I watched her shoulders, her hair held back with hairpins, and I hated her. Did my father know what she was doing to me?

It was a warm day, and fog was still dissipating from the fallow fields; despite the sound of fighting on the horizon, the world had an air of imperturbable serenity.

All of a sudden I couldn't keep going, starving and exhausted as I was. We had been on the road for an eternity, and I was stopping every few steps. Ursula turned round and snapped impatiently, 'So, are you going to move, or do I have to drive you like a mule?' As she twisted abruptly, her handbag fell open, and the clasp caught me full in the face, breaking the skin. It was all so quick that I didn't realise what had happened until I felt blood running down my cheeks. I dipped my finger in it, stared disconcertedly at my finger and realised I was fainting.

When I came to, I found myself sitting against the trunk of a tree with my stepmother glaring at me. 'Are you feeling any better?' she asked. I nodded, contemplating the yellow bud of a dandelion and feeling incredibly tired.

Eventually Ursula said, in a tone quite unfamiliar to me, 'I can't cope with you any more, Helga. Two children are more than I can handle, I had no idea how hard it would be.' She spoke with such disconsolate frankness that I felt an absurd bond of solidarity. I said gently, 'I will be good at my new school.' I wanted to make her happy. She turned away, touched by what I had said. Finally we set off again, arriving fifteen minutes later at our destination.

It was a two-storey building surrounded by greenery. Before the war, Eden had been a district devoted to intensive fruit-growing, but now almost the entire male workforce was at the front, and as the women were unable to do all the work themselves, many of the trees stood languishing.

The school impressed me immediately.

We were welcomed by the headmistress, a woman in her forties with kind eyes but a severe manner, and I took to her instantly. She introduced us to Dr Löbig, the school psychologist, who made a good impression on me as well. Dr Löbig was pink and plump, with a motherly smile.

We were led to the dining room, where about fifteen children were seated at a long table. I was sat down in front of a steaming plate of something I didn't recognise, a kind of purée of cabbage and potatoes scattered with a powder I later learned was soya. I didn't greatly care for the taste of the powder, but I still gulped down the lot without pausing to draw breath. My stepmother had been invited to the headmistress's table. The children stared at me curiously, and, once my plate was clean, I stared back. After the soup there was an apple as well, and I felt very satisfied; there was far more on the menu here than there was in Berlin. Then an older girl clapped her hands and exclaimed, 'Everyone out into the garden!' The room emptied in an instant. My stepmother, the headmistress and Dr Löbig all stayed inside. The headmistress finished off some formalities with Ursula, while Dr Löbig asked me some questions that I tried my best to answer correctly. The headmistress wanted to give my stepmother some apples and potatoes. Then she said calmly to me, 'Cheer up, Helga, it's time to say goodbye to your mother. She has to get back to Berlin.'

'I was about to say, "She's not my mother," but I managed to bite my tongue. Ursula hugged me and said, 'When you're better, I'll come and get you.' I didn't know what I was supposed to be cured of, but I didn't reply. I just nodded, trying to smile as nicely as I could. My stepmother left, and in spite of everything I felt a small, absurd pain at our parting. Then the headmistress took my hand and led me into the garden. I saw two swings and a long slide. Two children were digging in a big sandpit. The headmistress said to them, 'This is Helga, she's going to be staying with us. Be nice to her.' The two children looked at me; then one of them handed me a spade and asked, 'Do you want to play?'

I burst into tears.

IV

I remember Eden Boarding School with warm gratitude. Apart from the daily sessions with Dr Löbig, which took place in a brightly decorated attic room, I never had a sense of being in an institution of any kind. We were treated firmly but affectionately, and our mistakes were corrected spontaneously because we were part of a community, and everyone took part in its educational project. Sometimes giving people responsibility can work miracles. We gained self-confidence and the rougher edges of our characters were smoothed. We had an open, devoted relationship with the headmistress, who was a passionate anti-Nazi and made no secret of the fact. She despised Hitler for his fanaticism, his racial hatred, his crazed anti-Semitism. But despite these good relations, life in Eden was not easy.

Apart from anything else, the war was present there, too, with all the fear, uncertainty and hunger that came with it. The headmistress made extraordinary efforts to guarantee the survival of her community, but we all had to play our parts. We weren't subjected to heavy bombing raids, but there was still a serious sense of instability, of imminent catastrophe.

The headmistress, along with her own elderly parents and the boarders, tended to some of the fruit trees but lamented the fact that much of the harvest had to be given up as part of the war effort, and that the rest was pilfered by the starving populace.

Spring and summer passed. I had settled in well, but hunger remained a serious problem. Each of us was allowed a single slice of bread per day; apart from that, we were given soup, not identified more specifically than that, mixed with soya powder. Each small egg was supposed to feed five of us.

One of the boarders was a member of the Bahlsen biscuit-making family and regularly received packages of the most delicious confectionery but refused to share anything with anyone. He used his hoard to barter, in order to get out of doing various jobs. One day he struck a deal with me to clean the courtyard, for which I earned two chocolate biscuits, but when the headmistress found out what was going on, I was punished.

The headmistress put us to work alternately in the garden, in the orchards, in the kitchen or in the shed where jam was made, but she also sent us to the main road to collect horse-dung to be used as fertiliser. I was usually paired up with Hans, a boy two years older than me who played the accordion. Hans pushed the wheelbarrow while I scraped the manure from the road with a shovel. Every now and again we saw armoured transports passing or heard the rumble of anti-aircraft fire in the distance, and then we remembered there was a war on.

One day we passed beyond the boundary fixed by

the headmistress. All of a sudden, in a field near the road, we saw two men in shirt-sleeves stirring large pots. Hans set the wheelbarrow down and stared at the men as though hypnotised. Then one of them saw us and shouted something in a language we didn't understand. He beckoned us over, and my heart froze. I was afraid they might hurt us, perhaps shoot us. Knees trembling, we obeyed. Other men appeared from behind a slope. One of them invited us, in German, to come over to the pots, which had semolina porridge boiling in them. Then another man poured butter and jam into the pots and stirred them vigorously. Finally they gestured to ask us whether we were hungry. We nodded automatically, our minds blank with terror. Then one of the men filled two bowls with the sweet, greasy porridge and handed them to us. Unable to believe what was happening, we devoured the porridge in a flash before the men's amused eyes. To me it felt like a dream, yet I really was filling my belly! Finally they gave us some black bread and waved us on our way. We could hardly get over our astonishment. Hastily pushing the wheelbarrow around the next corner, we started on the bread. It was moist and sweet, so moist that you could have rolled it into little marbles. Reluctantly we decided to take a little back to the headmistress.

But she wasn't at all pleased and she never sent anyone to the road to collect dung again.

We later found out that German troops were stationed nearby, along with some Russian mercenaries who had been recruited into the *Wehrmacht*. Those strange people hadn't seemed so bad to me.

Every now and again I was gripped by a desperate feeling of abandonment and I felt different from the other children, who received letters from their families and sometimes even had visits from them. When the headmistress and Dr Löbig saw that I was unhappy, they went to great lengths to comfort me. Sometimes I hid in the shed, brooding behind the door among the pots, rakes and hoes; I had had no contact with my family since my arrival. However, during those days I learned to walk on stilts! Despite frequently falling headlong and grazing my knees, I persevered; I wanted to be the best girl in the school.

In September 1943 I started attending classes, but although I very much wanted to learn to read and write, my output was rather sparse. I was unable to concentrate. I felt fidgety all the time and was unsettled by the big hall in which three classes were taken by a single teacher. It was always extremely chaotic. The teacher was old and disagreeable, and she held her stick at the ready to bring it down on our fingers. I always yelled more loudly than the others, because I remembered being beaten by my step-mother, and consequently the teacher took a dislike to me. She started giving me so much homework that I was soon unable to perform my duties in the vegetable garden, the orchards or the kitchen, and my school-mates started calling me a lazy-bones. I felt unjustly accused and became more and more miserable. My situation was aggravated by a form of nervous insomnia. I lay for entire nights with my eyes wide open; sometimes I got up, went to the bathroom, climbed on to the toilet seat, opened the window and listened to the vast darkness beyond the orchards, pierced every now and again by intersecting beams of light from the anti-aircraft emplacements. I often fell asleep just when it was time to get up, but fortunately I was allowed to sleep on. When I awoke, seeing that the others had gone to school without me, I felt terribly guilty, and went to the orchards or the kitchen to make myself useful. When the others came back, I was too ashamed to show my face. So I hid under the elder bush at the bottom of the vegetable garden, comforted by the damp warmth of the stagnant air that hung between the bean-poles and the lettuces.

The headmistress listened to the BBC to learn about the progress of the war, and one day I heard her reporting rumours about Berlin that frightened me. She said the city had been reduced to ruins and that the population was dying of hunger. I thought of my brother and felt profoundly anxious.

V

Berlin, autumn 1944

At the end of the summer of 1944, a woman came to
the school saying she was Aunt Hilde. I didn't
recognise her.

'Don't you remember me?' she asked severely,
arching one eyebrow. I had a better look: a little hat
with a veil (how I hated little hats!), eyes the colour
of lead, a mole on the end of her nose, very thin lips
painted scarlet, a dress patterned with bright little
flowers which clashed wildly with the general mood
of catastrophe. I stammered 'Maybe . . . that is . . .
well . . . I don't know.' Giving me a remote and
frosty smile, she said, 'I've come to take you back to
Berlin.'

She had caught me off guard. I glanced in confusion
at the headmistress, who looked perplexed. But Hilde
went on: 'Wouldn't you like to see Peter again?'

'Yes!' Peter was a little scrap of love I nurtured in
my heart like a nestling. Peter was certainty, Peter was
family.

'Then get your things together,' Hilde ordered, as
though exploiting a moment of weakness.

I looked at her indecisively, uneasily, torn between yes and no, between the desire to see Peter again and the fear of going back to Berlin. People were saying awful things about the city, that there was destruction, hunger, desperation and air-raids day and night.

Once again I peeped at the headmistress, who looked seriously at Hilde and asked, 'Are you sure this is the best thing for Helga?'

'What do you mean?' Hilde asked coldly.

'I'm thinking of the situation in Berlin,' the headmistress replied.

'My dear lady,' Hilde explained, scratching her mole, 'I am here on the instructions of my sister, Helga's mother. Under the circumstances I don't believe that either my opinion or yours carries any weight whatsoever, do you?'

The headmistress shrugged impotently and said to me, 'Go and get your things, darling. I have some details to sort out with your aunt.'

Head bowed, I went up to the dormitory and got my little case. The other children watched me. I had a lump in my throat and began to cry. Hans murmured, 'You're lucky you're going home, but I'd like you to stay here,' at which point I started crying in earnest. In the little entrance hall everyone had assembled to say goodbye, including the cook, the headmistress's old parents, the headmistress herself and Dr Löbig. They all hugged me while I choked back my tears. I was afraid, especially of Hilde, who was so cold and authoritarian! Abruptly she picked up my little case and declared: 'Right, then, time to go, we have a long journey ahead of us.'

The headmistress said to her, 'I'd like to give you some of our jam.'

Hilde put the case back down and replied brightly, 'Oh, I'd be delighted, you can't get a thing in Berlin these days!'

While we waited, I was in torment. I had helped to make that jam, I had spent ages stirring the pans while Hans played the accordion! When the headmistress returned with a little jar I burst into tears again. Hilde whispered: 'Might one know why you cry all the time?'

'I am not crying!' I protested. Gulping, wiping my nose and squeezing my eyelids together as though wringing out a wet handkerchief, I stopped crying.

Finally we went out into the courtyard, and I saw my stilts propped up against the wall of the shed. 'I want my stilts!' I cried, remembering not only the terrible falls and the bloody knees but also the intense happiness of walking on them.

Hilde flashed me a look of contempt. 'Don't talk nonsense, Helga!' she exclaimed as she dragged me towards the gate.

'I want them!' I insisted, and dug in my heels like a mule. I didn't really want the stilts, I wanted to stay at the school; I didn't want to be cast out of Eden to end up in the depths of Hell!

Once again I burst into floods of furious, rebellious, impotent tears. Giving me a handkerchief, Hilde exclaimed, 'That's enough of your snivelling!' She was very annoyed. She shook her head, she shook her little hat, and she dragged me towards the gate, which clanged shut. The sound reverberated in my heart.

Even before we started walking, I was exhausted with weeping.

We turned into the main road. It reminded me of Hans, the wheelbarrow, the horse-dung and our encounter with the Russians who ate semolina porridge and made sweet black bread; I wept again. The road was very busy: a column of lorries full of women and children, carts and covered wagons, prams laden with bundles and cases, was heading inexorably westwards. Refugees or people fleeing the Russians.

After an interminable walk we reached the *S-Bahn* station, where we were told that the last train had left a few hours before. We prepared ourselves for a long wait by eating the two slices of bread the headmistress had given us for the journey.

Finally a train arrived. It approached slowly, almost nervously; its sides were dented, its windows gaping. An impatient crowd rushed towards it: soldiers, officials, Hitler Youth, a few civilians. Hilde and I managed to board a carriage. I was lost among all the legs in uniforms and boots. Hilde shouted, 'Where are you?' I pushed my way into people's bottoms and received kicks and punches in return but finally found myself by Hilde's side again. She had lost her hat, and her lipstick had been smudged all the way to her cheekbones, making her look like a clown.

The train set wearily off. The carriage was freezing, an icy wind blasting through the shattered windows. I was terrified, numbed by the cold and very thirsty.

A depressing scene passed by outside: the city resembled an enormous bonfire.

Soon the carriage was filled with smoke, and I started coughing. I wanted to go to the toilet, and I longed to return to Eden. We changed trains twice.

Finally we reached Steglitz station, where we were swept along by the crowd. An officer, shouting at the top of his voice, was rounding up a squadron of very young soldiers, some of them keen and euphoric, some of them stiff, anxious and lost. Standing on the station forecourt I tried to breathe deeply, but the air was filled with a heavy smell of burning. The unnatural heat made me shiver. I stared in confusion at the ashes covering the cobbles, unable to work out where they were coming from. But Hilde urged me on: 'Don't stand there like a statue, let's get a move on before the air-raid warning.' She gripped my hand in hers.

We passed by long terraces of bombed, smoking ruins. The footpath was scattered with broken glass. I slipped and fell, some splinters pierced my arm. Hilde snorted: 'Can't you be more careful?'

Then she told me we were not going to Friedrichsruher Strasse but to the family home, where I would find Peter, our stepmother and her father.

'My cellar is safer than yours,' she explained, adding out of the blue, 'My mother died last month.'

'Your mother?' I asked distractedly.

'Your grandmother. We were able to bury her in Lichtenberg cemetery.'

My grandmother? Ah, she meant my grandmother by marriage. I exclaimed rebelliously, 'My grandmother is in Poland!'

Hilde said acidly: 'Whether you like it or not, my mother was also your grandmother.'

I didn't dare to contradict her.

'She had a heart-attack during an air-raid,' Hilde explained. I nodded dispassionately, having only seen that 'grandmother' on four occasions. Noting my indifference, Hilde sighed, shook her head and said bitterly, 'It doesn't matter,' letting go of my hand. On the corner of Lothar Bucher Strasse, I asked her, 'Where is your house?' I could see nothing but ruins.

'It's the very last building.'

'I need a pee,' I whined.

She sighed again. 'All right, then, go ahead, what are you waiting for?'

'Where?'

'Well, here, where else, what's the problem?'

'I'm ashamed.'

'But no-one can see you!'

I hesitated. She smiled tiredly and turned to look towards the end of the street where her house was. I immediately crouched down and peed in a hole that reeked of sulphur, but at the same time something drew my attention. It was the torso of a teddy bear. I was about to pick it up when Hilde thundered, 'What on earth are you doing? You're not to bring home everything you find in the street!' And she dragged me away.

We had almost reached the door of the house when a woman ran towards us, shouting, 'Get away from here! Run to the shelter! They're coming!'

I looked up and saw a triangle of low-flying planes followed by other triangles; at the same time a chorus of wailing sirens went up. My heart leapt into my throat: the sirens had sounded too late, the planes had

49

already begun firing, and all hell broke loose. I was short of breath and thought I would collapse. Then a powerful blast of air hurled me against the door. Feeling as though I was falling into a deep ravine, I lost consciousness.

When I came to, I found myself lying on the ground with a loud roaring in my ears. Everything around me seemed to be flying through the air, fragments of brick, bits of tarmac, pieces of wood. Everything was shaking, the earth writhed and slumped, furrowed as though gashed open by a crazed ploughman. I saw Hilde lying at the door, arms slack, eyes closed, with a trickle of blood running slowly from her hairline to the corner of her mouth. She looked as if she was dead. The roaring was still all around us, and as I burst into terrified tears, a lashing rain of rubble crashed down on me like a hurricane. My mouth and nostrils filled with dust and sand, and I felt I was suffocating. I spat earth, blood and bits of brick. I tried to get up, but something was crushing me to the ground. I was asphyxiated by a kind of searing heat. My hands felt as though they been roasted. Finally, still spitting blood, I crept towards Hilde on my hands and knees. All of a sudden a sinister silence fell, even more terrifying than the din that had preceded it.

I reached Hilde and stared at her in astonishment, touching her chin gently. Suddenly she opened her eyes and gazed at me vacantly, murmuring, 'What happened?' Then her face sprang into life: 'Oh my God, are you injured?'

'I don't know . . .' I looked at my hands, my arms. There was blood, I was horrified. I choked back my nausea. Suddenly Hilde whispered, 'Please don't turn round . . .' But I turned round straight away and saw her. The woman who had shouted 'Run to the shelter!' She was lying not far from us in a pool of blood, headless. I vomited. I vomited my guts up. I vomited up all my horror at the world.

Meanwhile Hilde had struggled to her feet and was hammering on the door. 'Damnation!' she cursed. 'It must be jammed!' Finally someone opened the door, and a pair of arms pulled us inside. We went down a flight of stairs.

The cellar was dark and full of people who stared at us. There was no air. The first person I saw was my brother, and I immediately burst into tears again. In a broken voice I yelled, 'Peter, I'm back!'

He looked at me uncomprehendingly in the flickering light of a lamp and then glanced questioningly at our stepmother, who said, 'It's your sister, Helga.'

He went on staring at me, rubbing the tip of his shoe against his calf. Peter, thin and less curly-haired, Peter, taller and not as chubby. Peter: my brother. He couldn't make head or tail of the situation, and stuck a finger in his nose.

'Helga?' he asked finally, tilting his head. Then I flew to him and hugged him. He started crying, and I cried with him. My hands touched an emaciated body. It broke my heart.

We all hugged each other. Hilde asked Peter, 'Have you been good, you little rascal?' He muttered, 'I threw up.'

I was happy to see my stepmother's father again. He

was tall and distinguished, with clear, intelligent eyes, grey hair with a parting, elegant if crumpled clothes. Who thinks about ironing in wartime?

Then an old man examined us carefully. 'You have only superficial injuries,' he declared. 'You are lucky. Fräulein Hilde, you could have died!'

Hilde said, 'It's a scandal, they sound the air-raid warning when the planes are already overhead!' At that moment the cacophony of machine-gun fire struck up again.

'They've come back, the swine,' said the old man. 'May God blow up the lot of them!'

Faces grew tense with anxiety, and with each explosion people opened their mouths and blocked their ears. This, I discovered later, stopped their eardrums bursting.

When the raid was over, we had our supper: bread and turnips. The bread was dry, and the turnips were withered. Our little jar of jam had been lost along with my suitcase in the inferno.

After our meagre supper, my stepmother put me to bed on the top of a rudimentary bunk bed. She asked me about Eden and told me about life in Berlin. Shortly afterwards my grandfather came to say good-night. 'Call me Opa,' he said kindly. 'I'm here if you need anything. Try to rest.' But I was too shaken. I was cold and felt lost and unhappy. Looking around me, I saw poor things and poor people in a gloomy cellar lit by a single oil lamp that cast gloomy shadows on the wall. An old woman, wrapped in an absurd black taffeta dress, was praying. 'Would you stop it?' an elderly man roared, glancing at her with exasperated reproach. But the old woman replied calmly, 'It would do you good, Herr Hammer, to communicate with the Lord.'

The man replied scornfully, 'A God who allows this war to happen doesn't deserve prayers!' And he spat on the floor.

'I'm still hungry . . .' I heard Peter murmur in the bed below mine.

'Go to sleep,' our stepmother replied in a fond and regretful voice.

'I want some bread!' Peter insisted.

'Go to sleep . . .' she repeated.

Finally, feeling terribly alone, I managed to nod off.

VI

When the sirens wail we all run to the cellar; when the all-clear sounds we go back to our flats. People are constantly tearing up and down the stairs, fretful, terrified and exhausted with hunger.

Hilde's flat still retains an air of past elegance despite the shredded wallpaper and crumbling walls. Explosions have shattered all the window-panes, which have been replaced by boards.

Through the cracked glass of a window overlooking Lothar Bucher Strasse, you can make out the black ruins opposite and the puddle of blood left by that poor woman who was hit by a shell so close to our front door. Look to the left and you can see a corner of an advertising column bearing the slogan *DER FEIND HÖRT MIT*: 'The enemy is listening.'

The flat is cold and dark, even in the daytime. We have to use oil lamps or candles. Even though I constantly feel weak, the forced inactivity is a torment. In Eden I went to classes or collected horse-dung from the road with Hans, or talked to Dr Löbig; I might have gone to pick windfalls with the others, or walked on my stilts, but here I have nothing to do except wait for the next air-raid warning. I can't go into the courtyard, because we're always in the line of fire; we can't even distract each other by chatting because Peter only wants to talk about bombs or the Führer, and when I suggest a game of hide-and-seek, he looks at me as though I'm a halfwit.

We are vegetating in a ghost town, without electric light or gas, without water; we are forced to think of personal hygiene as a luxury and of hot meals as abstract concepts. We are living like ghosts in a vast field of ruins, where the few remaining buses and trams cart us circumspectly around like animals bound for the slaughter, where the schools have no pupils, the shops no goods, the theatres no actors and the churches no congregations – because Nazism hates priests but also because the wide naves are being used as arms dumps – and where the few hospitals still standing are without water, electricity, medicines and doctors. A city where nothing works apart from the telephones that sometimes ring, glumly and point-lessly, beneath piles of fallen masonry.

At home, the toilet is blocked, and we have to use a bucket, which then has to be emptied in the courtyard. We risk death to bury our excrement.

The kitchen is dominated not by the smell of food but by the stench of burning that mingles with the nauseating stench of corpses which lie decomposing in the streets.

I am concerned about Peter: he shows no interest in playing but is utterly fascinated by anything to do with the Führer. He knows the names of Hitler's closest collaborators, his personal doctor, his favourite food and his various headquarters, which

Peter lists with his funny hissing 's': the Wolfschanze, the Adlerhorst, the Berghof, the Felsennest-Eifel, the Reich Chancellery and so on . . . His information comes to him first-hand, from Hilde.

One rainy afternoon, when we have just got back from the shelter after a heavy air-raid, Peter drags me into the chilly dining room to tell me something important: 'Do you know we're going to the Chancellery bunker?' He stands there, legs apart, fists on hips and eyes bright, waiting for my reaction.

'Who's going?' I ask without a great deal of interest.

'You and me!'

'Why would we want to go there?' I wonder, not taking him too seriously; every now and again he enjoys making up nonsense just to provoke a reaction.

'To eat liver sausage and see the Führer!' he exclaims agitatedly, standing there in his lederhosen, with his wayward tuft of hair and his cheeky little nose, his wartime pallor, disappointment on his face at my refusal to shriek with delight.

'Who told you that?' I mutter, reluctantly falling for his game.

'Aunt Hilde.'

I prick up my ears. If Hilde said it, it might be true. Working as she does at the Propaganda Ministry, it wouldn't be hard for her to book us in as 'special guests of the Führer', the term used for those privileged individuals who enjoy periods of 'respite' in the Reich Chancellery bunker; there is rumoured to be an abundance of food there.

'When are we going?' I ask, stroking the gleaming

surface of the piano, which has been left miraculously undamaged.

He shrugs: 'Soon!' He's offended by my lack of enthusiasm.

'Is Opa coming too?' I ask.

'Just you, me and Mutti!' Peter snorts sullenly. Now he has decided to punish me by feeding me information in dribs and drabs.

But I say stoutly: 'I don't want to go to the Chancellery bunker, and I don't want to see the Führer either!'

When I was in Eden I heard horrible things about the Führer; the headmistress didn't mince her words. She maintained that Hitler was dragging Germany towards disaster, that he was a crazed megalomaniac; that he hated black people, ballet dancers, poets and priests, and burned the books of writers hostile to Nazism. The headmistress said that Hitler was persecuting the Jews even outside Germany, that he was having the Gestapo arrest them along with their children before taking them to concentration camps. The same thing had happened to her sister. A widow, she had been arrested with her two daughters, twins barely three years old, and deported to a concentration camp in Poland, accused of polluting the Aryan race by marrying a Jew.

'No,' I repeat, 'I don't want to go to the Führer's bunker!'

'You're stupid!' shouts Peter.

'So are you!'

My brother stares at me in disbelief, his face growing grimmer and grimmer. He really can't imagine that someone might not share his passion for the Führer. In a voice filled with rage and rancour he says, 'Well, you're going to have to come with us, Mutti will order you to, you'll see!'

'I'm not going!' I shout, outraged by his over-bearing manner. 'I'm not going because the Führer is bad! I don't want to see the Führer because he sends children to concentration camps and makes people burn books!'

Peter gives me a worried look, as though I have shattered an idol, and protests furiously: 'Only Jewish children go to concentration camps, we aren't Jewish children!' And he starts kicking a table, rattling the already broken crystal on top of it.

'The headmistress at Eden said that no children should be sent to concentration camps!' I exclaim, aflame with fury. 'The headmistress said that no-one should be sent to them at all! The headmistress said that anyone who sends people to concentration camps is bad! I don't want to go to the Führer's bunker because the Führer is bad! He sends people to camps and their mothers too!'

Peter's neck twitches, and he shrieks, 'Mutti won't go to a concentration camp because she isn't Jewish! None of us are going to go to a concentration camp!'

'But no-one else should be sent there either!' I insist.

'Only Jews are!' He is whimpering by now.

'The headmistress said the Jews shouldn't,' I insist. 'No-one should be sent to camps, no-one!'

Peter looks at me in confusion, unable to grasp the point. Then he shrugs again and announces, 'Fine, then I'll go to the bunker with Mutti, and we'll eat your sandwiches as well as our own!' And he starts jumping up and down on the springs of an armchair, repeating, cheeky as a monkey: 'We'll eat your sandwiches too, and I'll tell the Führer you're a liar!' But all of a sudden he stops, pointing at a picture hanging crookedly from a cracked wall, and shouts disdainfully: 'Papa painted that, and you didn't know! Na-nana-na-na!'

'Really?' I murmur, crushed.

'You didn't know, you're an idiot!' And he thumbs his nose at me.

I burst stupidly into tears; at last a sign of my father! I stare at the painting, which shows two lions in the savannah. A feeling of warmth floods through me, and I shout the first thing that comes into my head: 'Isn't the lady lion beautiful!'

Peter jumps from the armchair, frowns, comes over to me, points a finger and shouts contemptuously, 'It's called a lioness, you silly ass!'

The haughtiness in his voice! He's right, of course, you do say 'lioness' and not 'lady lion', but he shouldn't have corrected me so nastily! Then I open my eyes wide to scare him, and brazenly deny the obvious: 'You're wrong, you say "lady lion"!'

'Lioness!' he snarls.

'Lady lion!'

'You silly goose, you say "lioness"!' he shouts.

'Lady lion!' I have tears in my eyes.

He gives in, but he spoils my victory. 'Anyway, you're a goose, Mutti says so too!' he exclaims in a voice of childish contempt, and leaves me on my own in the cold dining room. I am hurt and powerless.

The truth is that my brother doesn't love me. My long absence has erected a wall between us, has erased any instinctive affection in him, as though he has been drained by the grave and threatening events around us. The world can give me nothing now because it has already taken everything away: my childhood, my mother, my father, my grandfather, my brother. What am I left with? Hunger, thirst, fear, cold, loneliness.

In the cold drawing room, I walk over to my father's painting and stare at it hopelessly. What I really long to do is to plunge my nails into the canvas and scratch the surface away. I long to scratch until my nails are worn away, to see if there is anything of my father underneath, a reference, a reflection. I long to pull the painting from the wall and dig among the colours, separate the reds from the greens to uncover some gesture of my father, an echo of his breath, his heartbeat. I climb on to a chair, determined to possess the canvas, to rummage among the grass of that peaceful savannah, to shout to the lions, 'Tell me something about the man who painted you so lovingly!' But at the last minute I get a grip and merely stroke the canvas gently, respectfully. The surface is rough to the touch, and I feel a faint warmth flowing into my finger-tips; I start to cry. But it is only an illusion. The canvas is silent, and the lions go on watching impassively, motionless in the sun.

I go into the chilly kitchen, where Peter is showing off to our stepmother. He is performing one of his familiar routines, in which he imitates the speeches of Goebbels in a singsong voice as though they were playground chants: '... we will make those imperialist warmongers, those subhuman Bolsheviks ... we will make the enemy look upon their total defeat ... an eye for an eye, a tooth for a tooth ... final victory ... *Kameraden!*' He likes to accompany his recitation with the affected gestures used by power-crazed politicians, and to make his voice low and slyly seditious; and of course he is careful not to omit the concluding cry of '*Heil Hitler!*' How different he is from the children I knew at Eden!

Once the show is over, Ursula laughs and applauds. The kitchen is filled with the stench of burning and of corpses, which penetrates everything. Our stepmother is pleased with Peter because she has managed to mould him as though he were her own son; I am plainly the daughter she would never have wanted in a thousand years. I can't forgive her for what she has done to my brother! She has filled his head with the concept of a master race, of which Peter, the little cherub, now imagines himself to be a perfect example.

'I'm hungry!' Peter announces, propping his little fists on his hips.

'It isn't evening yet. If I give you your bread ration now, what will you have left for your supper?'

'But I'm hungry now!'

'A true German shows self-control, Peter!'

Another topic in which Peter shows an unhealthy interest is bombs. They seem to have a sinister hold on his imagination despite the fact that, in the shelter, he seemed to understand the danger they represented. Back in the flat, on the other hand, he enjoys going into minute detail about their destructive capacity, hoarding the information he was given by a deserter who infiltrated our cellar some months ago and who kept his submachine-gun trained on us for several days. Ever since then, Peter has been telling everyone about various murderous devices – incendiary bombs, demolition bombs, phosphorus bombs (an English speciality) and the Soviet mortars, the so-called 'Stalin organs', notorious for their ear-splitting whistle.

One other topic that obsesses Peter, although in a rather confused way, is the Jews, a subject that worries me too.

Our childhood was haunted by brutal anti-Jewish propaganda, and we witnessed expressions of anti-Semitism every day. Even as very small children, we had seen the shattered windows of Jewish shops, the shutters scrawled with the word *Jude*. People uttered this word cautiously, timidly, with embarrassment or fear, as though it referred to a contagious disease; sometimes they said it with contempt, the product of a propaganda campaign which maintained that 'the poisoner of all nations is international Jewry'. We all know that the Jews are forced to wear a star pinned to their chests, that Hitler has had the synagogues burned down, that Jews have been forbidden to grow their beards. Everyone is vaguely aware that the Gestapo seeks out Jews wherever they may be, to arrest them and deport them to concentration camps, and everyone has been given ample warning that those who hide Jews will be shot, while denouncing them may bring great benefits. People deny their Jewish relations and sever the firmest friendships with people suspected, however remotely, of being of Jewish origin. Word is even heard of children denying their parents or, worse, denouncing them to the authorities, and, conversely, of people risking their lives to protect or hide Jews. Why will my brother not open his eyes?

My father is officially missing now, and nothing is known about our other relatives. Ursula has phoned the villa in Tempelhof several times, but there has been no answer.

We are consumed with hunger; all of us are nervous and emaciated. People are scouring the city in search of the food warehouses that supply the *Wehrmacht*, the SS, the Führer's entourage and some well-to-do families. Whenever such a warehouse is discovered, it is plundered mercilessly, even if it means killing anyone who opposes the raid. The populace has become fatalistic, scornful of danger; they are willing to risk their lives for a slice of bread or a spoonful of sugar; but weeks can go by before the search for food is successful. All the cats in the city have ended up in the pot, and people are devising the most ludicrous ways to catch the poor sparrows that flutter about the courtyards or among the rubble. They are almost tempted to eat the sewer rats that are growing disgustingly fat as they feed on corpses.

On one occasion my stepmother came back with about twenty turnips; for three days we ate nothing but turnips, and we all went down with dysentery. Every now and again Hilde brings us something from the Ministry shop, but even that is becoming more and more difficult.

A few days ago, as he was emptying the slop bucket

from the cellar in the courtyard, Opa was injured by a glass splinter, and almost bled to death because no doctor could be found. When our stepmother took him to hospital, the nurses laughed, saying they couldn't waste their time on anything so insignificant. Fortunately, the bleeding stopped spontaneously, but Opa was very weak for a long time afterwards.

If we want to fetch water, we have to go to the fountains or pumps, where terrified queues form, presenting far too easy a target for the enemy. Often the queues are mown down by shells or mortar-fire, or by lightning artillery attacks.

When we are in the flat, we always keep one ear open for the sirens; the moment they start to wail, we drop whatever we are doing and run to the shelter. Our suitcases are always packed with the things we want to save if the house collapses. Hilde wants to salvage her mink and her vacuum cleaner; our stepmother her mink and her silver, as well as her jewels; Opa his documents, a telescope, a precious camera, a travelling alarm clock, a gold watch, his late wife's jewels, two little oil paintings bought in 1936 at an auction in London and a few clothes. Peter wants to save his teddy bear, Teddy, showing a degree of tenderness at odds with his nature as a 'little German, a stranger to weakness and cloying sentiments'.

It is very hard spending so much time in the cellar, all crammed in together. The bucket that serves as our toilet, located at the end of a long and gloomy corridor, gives off the most disgusting odour. There is one old man who would rather soil himself than go all the way to the bucket. As a result the stench we breathe is indescribable. Because we are permanently short of water, the wretched man can't even have a good wash.

Recently the air-raid warnings have started coming in quick succession, giving us no respite. We are all in a very sorry state. Opa has a painful swollen knee, but we have no painkillers, and Hilde has not been able to find any either, even though she has put in direct requests to the Ministry. My stepmother is suffering from bilious colic and wraps her belly with woollen shawls, seeking comfort in massages she is given by Frau Köhler, the concierge of our building. I have scabs on my head, and Peter often vomits yellow foam. Whenever I get up from a chair or out of bed, I immediately feel faint.

Opa has a radio, although this is strictly forbidden. We listen in secret to news from the front, and to the BBC's German broadcasts. We can also pick up bulletins from the anti-aircraft service. There are blackouts and a curfew.

I feel lonely and unhappy. I want to go back to Eden! I want a blue sky, not one filled with ominous black flying-machines. I want to breathe air that doesn't smell of corpses. I want nights that don't explode over my head.

I want to see the sea. They say it's big, blue and pure. I want to see a beach. They say the beaches on the Baltic Sea are white, with soft dunes and, beyond them, rows of green pines. They say that in peacetime people go on holiday. I want to go on holiday! I want to go to the seaside! Instead we're going to the Chancellery bunker. Underground! A holiday for moles.

I told Hilde I didn't want to go, but she just got angry. She said I didn't know how lucky I was; my stepmother said I was ungrateful. Even Opa was able to look on the bright side: 'At least they'll fill your stomach,' he said.

Peter's enthusiasm wanes slightly when he hears that Ursula won't be able to come with us because Opa has tonsillitis, and she doesn't want to leave him on his own. Hilde won't be able to help, because she has been sent on a special mission by the Ministry (she says this is actually a delicate piece of secretarial work that must be carried out on the spot). The vision of liver sausage has won Peter over; he is willing to go even if Mutti doesn't come too. There will be other children there, we've been told, and one of Hilde's childhood friends, Marianne, will look after us. I don't want to go, but it's not up to me.

VII

Berlin, December 1944

Lothar Bucher Strasse is completely deserted. An anaemic winter sun brushes gently across a ruined row of house-fronts. The street and the footpaths are pitted with craters of every dimension. And there are piles of rubble everywhere, the remains of blackened walls, façades whose windows resemble blinded eyes. The air is ice-cold and makes our bones creak.

Opa has a good-quality pre-war woollen overcoat. My stepmother wears a handkerchief wound up like a turban to hide her dirty hair; without water there can be no hygiene, and without hygiene no dignity.

Peter is wearing his little shorts and his padded jacket. A light-coloured jacket, a dark face; he's decided he doesn't want to go to the bunker without his Mutti.

'A true German shows courage in every situation,' says our stepmother. 'What are you frightened of?'

'You come too,' grumbles Peter, his lower lip protruding.

'I've explained to you at least a thousand times why I can't come,' our stepmother replies, her turban slightly crooked.

I'm wearing a horrid heavy velvet dress that I hate, leather shoes with laces, and woollen socks that I hate as well. My coat is too small, I have the face of a hungry mouse, and my unruly hair has been cut into a pageboy by my stepmother, whom I also hate.

We're on our way to the Chancellery bunker. How could you not be happy to be able to spend time in such an important place, an underground city where hundreds of people from Hitler's entourage live and work, with all the offices, the kitchens, the laundry, the hospital, the dormitories and the space reserved for 'special guests of the Führer', a category that will soon include Peter and me? A privilege, that's what they say. It's a unique opportunity that we can't pass up, they repeat.

Ursula reminds Peter yet again: 'They'll give you fresh bread and liver sausage!' But Peter just shrugs.

'They'll give you toothpaste,' adds Opa. 'Think how much fun it will be to brush your teeth with toothpaste!'

'I'm more interested in the sausages!' Peter pipes up.

'And remember, Marianne will be with you,' our stepmother says, bending over backwards to reassure him. You'll see, you'll like her.'

'Won't!' Peter insists, kicking a shard of glass into a hole. At that moment the bus noses round the corner, advancing cautiously, stealthily. It is camou-flaged, a bus pretending to be an armoured car, a bus playing at war. The great brute comes to a stand-still, veering to avoid a crater. It belches smoke. It rumbles. Curious eyes observe us from the windows. Other 'special guests of the Führer', other privileged individuals. Peter pulls faces at them.

A young woman with Gretel braids gets out of the bus and quickly greets Opa and our stepmother. This must be Marianne: a hard, striking Teutonic beauty.

'Peter doesn't want to go to the bunker,' our stepmother declares, with a disapproving glance at the ungrateful little monster, who rolls his eyes in reply.

'Oh, what nonsense!' the young woman exclaims, picking Peter up like a parcel and putting him on the bus despite his kicking and loud remonstrations. Stepping back out of the bus, she says to me, 'You get on too, see if you can calm the earthquake.' I like Marianne's brisk attitude, so I hastily say, 'Goodbye!' and wave to Opa. 'Enjoy yourselves!' he encourages me, looking emotional as he struggles to maintain his dignity in his crumpled coat. I run towards the bus and climb the high steps, trying to display graceful energy in front of Gretel-Marianne, who is wrapped in a military coat that adds to her dependable allure. I join Peter, who is kicking the seat; then he breathes on the window and draws something that looks like a bomb with his finger. Marianne boards the bus as well and tells Peter to wave to Opa and Ursula, but he looks down and shakes his head. I give one final wave, and we set off.

The vehicle groans, screeches over rubbish, shards of glass, bricks and cobbles, rattles along the broken tarmac. We turn a corner. More ruins and grey, sad, plastery rubble; along a short path between two rows of box hedges lie corpses lined up like sardines, two of them headless. A kind of acid hiccup rises up from my stomach, and I swallow hard to keep from vomiting.

Peter continues to protest, attracting the attention of the other children; he thumbs his nose at them. Luckily, after one final cry of 'and I'm not coming', he goes to sleep on my shoulder. Marianne tells the driver, 'That's everybody, Herr Klug, we can head for the Chancellery now.'

I look out of the window again, the dreadful spectacle drawing me back. For weeks we haven't moved from Lothar Bucher Strasse, from a mad succession of air-raid warnings and all-clears, of terror and relief, so I feel an urgent and irrepressible need to understand what has been happening else-where. But what I see horrifies me. All that meets my eye are grim ruins and endless piles of rubble. After a while we come across a street in flames, and the sky becomes tinged with purple. The bus turns abruptly to the left and creeps along the tramlines to ensure that the crumbling façades don't fall on us. The vehicle fills with smoke and a smell of ash that dries the throat; outside it is raining ashes.

We continue on our way. Agitation is mounting in the bus.

Everywhere there are bits of wreckage, overturned trams riddled like colanders; an emaciated horse pulls a cart laden with corpses.

Corpses, corpses, rubble and buildings in flames: there seems to be nothing else in the city. In the bus the children are shrieking with fear. The two children sitting next to their own mothers are being calmed by them; the rest are dependent on Marianne. In the confusion Peter has woken up and, looking around him in bewilderment, has decided to seek refuge against my coat, whispering, 'I want to go home . . .'

I throw my arm around my brother's thin shoulders and go on looking out the window as though hypnotised. What sort of world am I living in? And what has become of Berlin, whose glorious past Opa once praised to the skies? It used to be a splendid, vibrant city, with millions of inhabitants working, producing and organising their lives with Teutonic perfection. A wealthy city with brightly lit streets, ostentatious window displays and elegantly dressed people walking along the Kurfürstendamm or Unter den Linden. People crowding into the restaurants, cafés, cinemas, theatres and concert halls. People cheering at sporting events in the Titania Palace. People courting, getting married, having children and raising them on the soundest principles. A modern city with an efficient underground train service and an equally functional elevated railway. What has happened to turn the place into a vast cemetery?

Near the Brandenburg Gate we run into a road block. A group of SS men are waving shovels in the air. The driver, Herr Klug, snorts: 'Shit!' He is elderly and wears a threadbare uniform with leather elbows patches. His hair is cut high above the white nape of his neck, and his bony shoulders slump exhaustedly over the big steering wheel. An SS man comes over to the door, pulls it open abruptly, climbs aboard the vehicle and shouts '*Heil Hitler!* Papers and passes, please!' Marianne isn't at all upset. She gets calmly to her feet and hands him an envelope. The SS man examines it minutely. He is very young, with eyes so pale they could be made of ice. He is so tall that his head touches the roof of the bus, and his uniform fits as though it had been stitched on to him. A worried silence has fallen.

Peter raises his head, stares at the SS man, murmurs, 'I'm not coming,' and huddles against my coat once again.

The SS man is satisfied. He shouts: 'Everyone in their seats!' Then he shouts, '*Heil Hitler!*' and jumps down from the vehicle. 'Bastards!' Herr Klug exclaims.

'Could you please keep your tongue in check!' Marianne reproaches him.

'Keep those bastards in check, more like!' growls the driver and starts up the engine.

The bus sets off once more towards the Brandenburg Gate, which stands out against a scaly sky whose innocent blue is drowned out by the scarlet of the flames. A few minutes later we stop again: we are there.

We all peer out, curious to see the famous Reich Chancellery, but I see nothing that matches my expectations.

The bus spews waves of smoke that rise to the windows: two sentries ignore us. They are tall, blond boys, pure Aryans, just the way the Führer wants them.

After telling us to be quiet, Marianne gets off the bus and heads towards a large front door; Herr Klug gets out too, to stretch his legs. I see him waving his arms to warm himself up; puffs of steam come from his mouth. When he comes back we besiege him: 'So where's the Reich Chancellery?'

He rests his elbows on the steering wheel and points with his chin towards a ruined building: 'That's it there, but that's the old one. It wasn't big enough for the Führer.'

We see only a ruin whose gloomy and wounded appearance is in perfect accord with the rest of the bombed city. Peter murmurs disappointedly: 'I don't want to go in there!' and starts shrieking. 'Be quiet!' shouts one of the mothers. 'How badly behaved you are, my boy!' At which Peter shrieks all the louder.

All that remains of the old Chancellery is the façade, which seems to have been seriously damaged. In front of it, and on top of what used to be flowerbeds, stretches a heap of rubble at which sparrows peck industriously.

What has remained standing, however, is the imposing outline of the new Chancellery, with its massive square columns and the little balcony at which the Führer liked to appear to greet the crowds that welcomed him with shouts of '*Sieg Heil!*'

Marianne comes back, waving the documents and letting us know that everything is in order. She pokes her head into the bus and says, 'Come on, everyone out and let's run to the bunker!' We are all very excited. I clutch Peter's hand, we get off the bus, we follow Marianne and are astonished to witness the spectacle of a vast iron gate rising slowly so that we can be swallowed up by the building. 'I'm not going in there,' announces Peter, who has abandoned the courage a German child is supposed to have and is kicking my foot.

I tighten my grip on his rebellious hand. As we start

down the concrete steps, we are hit by a gust of warm air.

A gleaming corridor opens up at the foot of the stairs; the lighting is cold, and some SS men lean against the reinforced concrete walls or sit on the ground cradling their submachine-guns in their arms. We walk down various corridors.

Heating pipes, the hum of fans. Indistinct voices come from all directions; we hear faint sounds that we can't identify, we see steel doors; I feel as though I am in a labyrinth.

Finally we stop at a checkpoint where a group of SS women are standing; they are all blonde, and they all look the same. Marianne has to sign a register, she chats with a girl with a Gretel face, and they swap jokes in Berlin dialect. Then we walk on. I feel dazed.

Telephones are ringing all over the place; I have a slight sense of panic, a faint attack of claustrophobia, but it soon passes. Peter has stopped kicking and is looking around him wide-eyed. We reach a kind of waiting room; Hitler stares at us from a huge portrait, moustache neatly trimmed, eye piercing as though trying to hypnotise us. Goebbels, on the wall opposite, wears a formal expression – he is the person in charge of Hilde's special missions. We are surrounded by large swastikas.

Another SS woman joins us and shouts, 'Heil Hitler!'; we reply 'Heil Hitler! She queries Marianne: 'Your journey was without incident?' 'Smooth as silk!' 'Come with me,' the SS woman says to us.

She leads us to a room full of bunk beds and iron

lockers and says, 'Put your things in there, please!'

I put my pyjamas and dressing gown in a drawer, along with the toothbrush I haven't used since my days at Eden. Opa said they are going to give us toothpaste. I'm curious to know what Peter will do with it: he doesn't even know what it is. There isn't a single tube left in the whole of Berlin.

'Wash your hands!' This new instruction is curt and military, so we make our way to a bathroom with lots of basins; we look like a herd of stupefied sheep. Fortunately Marianne stays with us, our sole point of reference. As soon as Peter is handed the tube of toothpaste he squeezes it in the middle and calls out scornfully, 'I'd rather have sausages!'

Marianne suppresses an amused smile and says, 'You'll have them too, but for now brush your teeth!'

After obeying, despite raising a thousand objections, and after trying to eat the toothpaste, my bossy little brother screams, 'I want to see the Führer!'

Marianne replies calmly, 'The Führer isn't here, and you must keep your voice down.'

'Where is he?' Peter has propped his little fists on his hips: he is scowling, fury in his eye, one foot tapping rhythmically on the ground, his lower lip trembling with irritation.

'The Führer is at the front, Peter.'

'But I've come here to see the Führer!' he insists disappointedly, yelling as he strikes a fist on the basin. The little despot is becoming an ogre.

'You'll get to see the Führer,' Marianne reassures him.

'When?'

'Soon.'

Now Peter is sure to want to stay in the bunker.

'Mealtime!' orders a voice.

We make our way to a refectory with long tables and wooden benches. Moisture glistens along the beams set in the concrete walls.

We arrange ourselves around the tables and start eating, stuffing our faces, devouring everything in a great rush as though we are worried that someone might suddenly order us to stop. Hitler looks down from yet another portrait, he looks down on slices of beef drenched in sauce and accompanied by burnt spaghetti, boiled potatoes, black bread, apple juice and syrupy tinned pears. As I try a pear, someone in the corridor shouts, 'A thousand units flying over Berlin!'

Peter murmurs dejectedly, 'Here too?'

'Don't worry,' says Marianne, who is sitting next to him. 'This bunker has a reinforced concrete roof three and a half metres thick, no bomb is going to touch a hair on your head.'

Peter relaxes and starts chewing again. Some of us feel sick, so we are taken to the bathroom, where we throw up. Then we come back and ask for a fresh portion of everything.

As we are having our dinner, the air-raid explodes above us, but the rumble of the bombs reaches us only faintly, like the sounds of a distant storm.

The days pass quickly. We sleep in the dormitory; the two mothers sleep with us, although Marianne is staying somewhere else.

Each morning a doctor examines us carefully,

checks our weight and gives us vitamins and medicines. The minute we arrived they tested us for tuberculosis. They even put us under a quartz lamp, and twice a day they force us to gulp down that repulsive substance called cod liver oil. There is also a recreation room with books for the older children and games for the little ones. Peter and Marianne often play dominoes, but I prefer to watch.

One day we are told that the Führer is coming to say hello, and Peter's face lights up. You would think he had been promised that he was going to meet Father Christmas!

They prepare us for the meeting with punctilious care. First of all, in the presence of the Führer you mustn't speak in a loud voice. If he should ask us anything, we are to reply, 'Yes, *mein Führer*' or 'No, *mein Führer*.' The Nazi salute is, of course, compulsory.

Peter can barely contain himself. It is his great dream to see the Führer. For him, the Führer is a landmark, he is the master, the father of the nation: for Peter, the Führer is God.

I'm less enthusiastic. I really didn't like what I heard about the Führer in Eden.

The fateful day arrives.

Peter and I are in the front row, both very tense; one little girl has developed a stomach-ache and been led away. Peter hops from one foot to the other, his face as pale as can be.

We are in a long hall draped all around with big swastikas. A number of chairs are arranged along the wall; at the end of the room a portrait of Hitler is flanked by clusters of German flags. The heat is damp and irritating. I am very nervous. Until the last moment we are told the same things over and over again: talk in a low voice, don't chatter in front of the Führer, give the Nazi salute without shrieking. We wait there as motionless as little lead soldiers. You could hear a pin drop.

But now we hear some noises and from a door on the left a group of young SS men comes in and stands in line along the wall opposite us. They are followed by a woman in uniform carrying a basket.

There is absolute silence in the room; my stomach contracts in a nervous spasm. And finally there he is, Adolf Hitler, the Führer of the Third Reich!

I become aware of a slight wavering among the ranks as the Führer makes his way slowly forward. We all jump to attention, raise our hands and shout 'Heil Hitler!'

We have yelled too loudly, and the Führer's face betrays a twitch of annoyance.

As Hitler advances towards us, I stare at him without breathing. I have heard so many things about him, from the most enthusiastic to the most contemptuous.

He walks slowly, his shoulders slightly bent, his feet dragging: I can't believe it! Can this be the man who once whipped crowds into a frenzy? What I see is an old man moving with difficulty. I notice that his head is trembling slightly, and that his left arm is dangling inertly along his side as though made of plaster. I am in a state of utter disbelief!

Hitler starts shaking hands with the first children in

the row, asking them brief questions by way of small-talk. I hear their voices, soft, shy, awkward, murmuring, 'Yes, *mein Führer*. No, *mein Führer*.' Finally it's my turn.

My heart misses a few beats and I blush violently. I am afraid I'm going to faint, to fall with a thud at the Führer's feet, and that's the last thing I want to happen.

Adolf Hitler holds out his hand to me and stares into my eyes. He has a penetrating gaze that makes me very uneasy. His pupils gleam strangely, as though there is a goblin dancing inside them.

The Führer's grip is weak, and I am perplexed. Can this really be the hand of the man guiding the fate of Germany? His hand is hot and sweaty, like that of a person with a fever. It feels unpleasant, and I am tempted to draw my own hand back, but I manage to control myself. Then I smile falsely, at the same time glancing at the SS men. Would they shoot me if they noticed my unease? You can't feel uneasy in front of the great Führer of the Reich! It's a crime! But they pay me no heed and keep their eyes fixed on the Führer, firmly clutching their submachine-guns.

Adof Hitler asks me, 'What is your name?'

'Helga,' I reply. I forget to say, *'mein Führer'*. There is a pause. I have a sense that Hitler is trying to find something to say, something like: 'Is the war causing you a great deal of distress?' or 'How is food distribution going in the city?' Instead he asks me, 'Do you like being in the Chancellery bunker, Helga?'

'Yes!'

It is a lie. I don't like being in the bunker because I

suffer from claustrophobia. It makes me feel as though I've been buried, locked in a coffin. The only thing that makes up for my sense of imprisonment is the food that arrives regularly, but apart from that I almost prefer the cellar in Lothar Bucher Strasse. I glance at the SS men again: have they spotted that I was lying to the Führer? Yes, I know, a 'special guest of the Führer' has a duty to feel good in the bunker, she is under an obligation of gratitude. But once again they ignore me, and I feel relieved. Then I look up and stare at Hitler's cap, with its eagle and swastika, before my eye slides down to a face with a greyish complexion that really bears very little resemblance to the portraits hanging in the bunker. The face I see before me is a damaged one. A dense network of wrinkles spreads around the eyes, and the cheeks are flabby. Only the well-trimmed moustache has a certain solidity among these disintegrating features.

When Hitler's hand withdraws from mine I feel a great sense of release. He reaches towards the basket, takes out a little bar of marzipan and holds it out to me. It's over. The Führer passes on, and it's my brother's turn.

'What's your name?'

'Peter!' he replies. Too loudly, with a hint of anxiety.

'How are you, Peter?'

Peter gives an interminable sigh, then shouts delightedly, spontaneously, impetuously, 'I'm fine, Herr Hitler! What a lovely buckle, Herr Hitler!'

It can't be happening, I feel as if I'm in a nightmare. Shattered, I look around and see Peter's impudent finger stroking the buckle on the Führer's belt! I think I'm dying. What's going to happen? Will the SS men fire a bullet into his little heart? I cast an anxious glance in their direction and notice with relief that one of them is trying to hide a smile of amusement. That puts my mind at rest. Then I hear the Führer's voice replying: 'When you are big, young man, you too will be able to have a buckle like mine.' The ritual with the marzipan follows, and then the Führer passes on. Once the first row is done, he says something like 'Good luck to you all.' Again we yell *Heil Hitler!*', again too loudly, and he leaves the room, followed by his bodyguards. The only one left is the woman, who goes on handing out the marzipan. The atmosphere eases.

Deutschland, Deutschland, über alles! So that's the great Führer of the Reich, the head of the German armed forces, the leader of us all! That's the man our destiny depends on. He has wished us good luck.

Heil Hitler!

VIII

Our stay in the bunker came to an end. We had put on weight, regained a little energy. We had become accustomed to an atmosphere of warmth – even if the reinforced concrete of the relatively recent construction did sweat with damp – and to the sense of security that comes from having three and a half metres of concrete over your head. I had even learned to keep my claustrophobia in check; some nights I managed to sleep for seven hours in a row, because down there we couldn't hear the sirens and the rattle of artillery was only faint.

We were crammed full of vitamins, saturated with cod liver oil and even tanned by the quartz lamp; we were in very good shape.

Our time in the bunker had weakened the memory of the reality outside, and I had even come to hope that things might have changed in the meantime, that the war was coming to an end and everything was going to get better.

Peter had finally got on everyone's nerves by constantly quoting the Führer. From the day of Hitler's visit, Peter spoke of nothing but his clothes: his trousers tucked into his gleaming boots, his cap with the eagle and the swastika, his impeccable military jacket and his belt with that famous buckle! Peter even talked about it in his sleep.

In the bunker I had overheard lively exchanges of opinion about the progress of the war, the Führer and the enemy. There were words and phrases that worried me, like 'Gestapo', 'KZ' (the abbreviation for 'concentration camp'), 'Jewish question', 'deportation'. Or 'Death's Head Units', 'Bolshevik enemy', 'secret army', 'battle for Berlin' and 'enemy', 'enemy' and, again, 'enemy'! I heard people talking about the Russians with visceral contempt. They called them a gang of primitive savages who stank of vodka and raped the women of the people they defeated. I also discovered that the two mothers who had been with us on the bus had once been hard-line Nazis and made no secret of the fact.

While the others were asleep and I was pretending to be, those two women held intense conversations that sometimes lasted until midnight. They were in the bunk bed next to mine, and I could hear every word.

I learned that they were the wives of so-called 'ordinary' SS, a lower-ranking category than the 'honorary' SS, whose members were for some reason illustrious, representative or influential, and that they were fanatically devoted to the Führer. They spoke as though the project of taking control of Europe and subduing inferior races was solidly under way, and they firmly believed that Germany had already won the war. But what made the strongest impression on me was the cold cynicism with which they spoke of the Jews. They called them 'filthy Jews' and hinted that

Hitler was planning to resolve the 'Jewish question' 'once and for all' in the concentration camps.

I heard things that terrified me and wondered what the Jews had ever done to Germany to allow two mothers to talk about them so contemptuously. It was in the bunker that I first heard talk of the 'extermination of the Jews', while the phrase 'Auschwitz concentration camp' issued from the mouths of the two women like a death sentence.

The children of those two mothers were equally fanatical. They told anyone who would listen that they couldn't wait to grow up so they could join the Hitler Youth and dedicate their lives to the Führer!

'Everyone ready?' Marianne asked, scrutinising the group as we prepared to leave the bunker.

We were ready. Gleaming shoes, brushed teeth and in our mouths the taste of the last spoonful of cod liver oil. Each of us had received a leaving present: a supply of sandwiches and a little bar of marzipan.

'I don't want to go!' Peter burst out. 'I want to wait for the Führer!'

'The Führer is at the front!' Marianne replied. 'Fighting the enemy.'

Peter frowned. Glaring enviously at two SS men who were getting bored in a corner, he protested, 'They're allowed to stay here!'

'Your mother's waiting for you at home,' Marianne reminded him.

'There are no liver sausages at home!' Peter replied with gastronomic logic.

'That's enough!' Marianne exclaimed impatiently. 'It's time to go!'

Peter made one last attempt to sabotage our departure, kicking out furiously and even trying to hurl himself to the ground. So Marianne threatened him: 'When I see the Führer I'm going to tell him how badly you behaved.' That was enough to convince the little rebel.

We walked back through the labyrinth of corridors, and at the checkpoint Marianne had to sign the register once more. Then came the final stretch: roaring fans, pipes, fire extinguishers. Marianne's heels clacked cleanly on the floor. And last of all, the stairs that carried us outside, the sliding door. We were back in the world!

A shiver ran through me. I greedily breathed in the air, which was at least fresh even if it was impregnated with a smell of burning, and looked up into the sky. It was an emotional moment.

'Out you go!' Marianne ordered.

We found Herr Klug, the driver who had brought us, back at the wheel.

'Bloody cold!' he complained, rubbing his hands.

'Everyone sit down and be quiet!' Marianne commanded.

'Just as long as the Ivans don't blow our heads off,' murmured Herr Klug.

'The bulletin was negative,' Marianne replied, 'stop panicking all the time, Herr Klug!'

Peter wanted to sit by the window. He breathed on the glass and drew a bomb with his finger.

The bus set off, Peter began to devour his

sandwiches and the marzipan, and there was no point suggesting that he leave something for the evening. When he had eaten the lot, he went to sleep.

In Hermann Göring Strasse, wind swept the scarred tarmac, a sky striped with red stretched away above a line of gloomy ruins. Black waves of smoke came from Potsdamerplatz.

The bus struggled onwards, fresh obstacles appearing every few metres. The familiar façades of bombed buildings slipped past, empty shells, violated and on the brink of collapse. Everywhere we looked we saw the wrecks of cars, eviscerated, bullet-ridden, burnt. Trams shattered, overturned, rusting. The carcases of animals, especially horses, some of them already partly decomposed, and, lined up along the walls, corpses as far as the eye could see.

I went on looking in disbelief, stunned, and as though I was waking from a dream I came back to reality with a jolt: the war was still raging, and nothing had changed! How had I been able to deceive myself?

I started weeping silently, little sobs I swallowed like bitter pills. So I could expect more nights in the cellar, I could expect to dash breathlessly down the stairs just as before. Once again there would be hunger, thirst, cold and terror! And that awful prospect suddenly struck me as unbearable. Where would I find the strength to face it all again? As I struggled against a profound sense of despondency, the driver cursed: 'The bastards!'

'What's up, Herr Klug?' Marianne asked from her seat.

'Planes in sight, that's what's up!'

Marianne ran to the front of the bus. Now I could see them too: a horrible triangle of planes directly above us.

We started to panic, but Marianne ordered us off the bus immediately.

Everyone started pushing towards the exit; the two mothers pulled the future members of the Hitler Youth along, hysterically shouting, 'Help! Hurry! Help!' Their cries rang out around the bus. Marianne said witheringly, 'Ladies, please control yourselves!'

Waking Peter abruptly, I dragged him from his seat. His eyes were wide and uncomprehending. Gripping his hand, I pulled him towards the door. He dug his heels in, and I had to tug him along. Striking my forehead against a metal bar, I felt a sharp pain, but I didn't let go of my brother.

The vehicle stopped abruptly, sending us tumbling on top of each other.

In a few minutes we were out of the bus, but all of a sudden Peter broke away from my grip and threw himself on the ground. Marianne picked him up, pointed to the doorway of a ruined building and started running. We all dashed along behind her.

We were running for our lives. The door was about thirty metres from the bus, and to reach it we had to skirt a long pile of rubble that provided no shelter. I ran with my eyes fixed on the door, getting a violent stitch in my side. I pressed a hand to it, but the movement threw me off balance. I stumbled into a crater and fell, hitting my jaw. I felt a tooth come out and land on my tongue. I spat it out, got back to my feet and continued running desperately. Now the planes were right above me: they were diving and firing. I thought the end had come. The stitch in my side grew more intense, leaving me breathless. The pain was so deep that I continued on all fours, but then I felt an even more searing pain in my calf. I wept dry tears. I couldn't see properly now.

I was on the point of giving up. Everything told me to let myself go. But then I felt two arms pulling me inside the doorway.

The certainty that I had made it revived me. I heard Herr Klug asking, 'Are you injured?' I pointed to my calf, and he had a look at it.

There was a great din all around us, mixed with the deafening rumble of the planes. I glimpsed Marianne as though she was wrapped in fog. She leaned towards me saying something, but the clamour drowned out her words. Herr Klug said, 'It's only a graze, little one, I'll tend to it when we're on the bus.' I whispered, 'My brother?' Herr Klug pointed towards Marianne, and it was only then that I saw my brother in her arms. I wept with relief; he was safe!

One of the other boys, Karl-Heinz, had been injured in the abdomen and was losing a great deal of blood. Herr Klug stopped up the wound as best he could.

'We've got to get him to hospital,' he said to Marianne.

When the cacophony had subsided, she read out her list of names. Everyone was present. Some of the children had been bruised but no more than that. The two mothers, who had escaped without so much as a scratch, went on weeping hysterically.

Once the raid was over, we cautiously stepped out of the doorway and made our way back to the bus. I took Peter's hand; he was calmer now. Marianne and Herr Klug picked up Karl-Heinz. The vehicle was battered; its roof was riddled with bullet-holes, and its windscreen was shattered. Hardly a window was left intact. The seats were scattered with fragments of glass.

'Think you can get that thing to go?' Marianne asked Herr Klug, as he continued to dab at Karl-Heinz's injury.

'It's got to go, damn it!' Herr Klug cursed, and sat down at the wheel.

The engine went hop-hop-hop and clop-clop-clop and didn't show the slightest sign of wanting to start. We all held our breath.

'Start, you bastard!' yelled Herr Klug. All of a sudden the engine changed its mind, and off we went.

We were all very upset. The bus was draughty and cold. Peter was clutching my coat and trembling. My calf was sore despite the fact that Herr Klug had covered it with a big plaster, and my sock was incrusted with blood.

The bus continued on its way among a thousand obstacles amid the shimmer of burning buildings; this must have been quite a heavy raid. As we pulled up in front of the hospital, we saw that one wing was on fire. Some nurses were running back and forth with stretchers. Herr Klug stuck his head out of the broken windscreen and shouted, 'We've got someone seriously injured on board, could anyone give us a hand?' But the nurses replied, 'Can't you see we're evacuating the burning wing?'

'To hell with it,' Herr Klug murmured and spat through the gaping hole in the windscreen. 'Boy or no boy, they don't give a damn.'

Marianne and Herr Klug carried Karl-Heinz into the hospital. They were gone for a long time. We were all left to freeze in the bus. When they returned, Herr Klug was cursing fit to bust. He said the hospital wouldn't take Karl-Heinz, and that Marianne had had to phone the Chancellery to find someone to put in an angry word. It was only then that those wretches had been persuaded to take the boy.

'Cheer up, everybody,' said Herr Klug, getting back behind the wheel. 'Who's getting out first?'

It was almost midday, and a scarlet haze filled the sky. I put my arm around my brother's frail shoulders and said tenderly, 'We'll soon be home.'

'I want to go back to the bunker . . .' Peter mumbled into my shoulder.

IX

The bus turns the wrong way down Lothar Bucher Strasse, but no-one raises any objections. The few cars moving about the deserted streets certainly aren't concerned about observing the traffic regulations, and in any case there is not a traffic policeman in sight; they're an utterly extinct species, like the firemen who should be putting out the fires caused by the phosphorus bombs. Nothing works any more: there are no postmen, no milkmen, not a single doctor to be found, and the emergency services, which had until recently been clearing the streets of corpses, have stopped answering the phone. A city once organised and functioning has abandoned its citizens to their own devices: there are no rights any more, and no duties either.

We say goodbye to Herr Klug, and Marianne walks us to the front door. She salutes us as though we were two soldiers, says, 'Right then, off you go, I want to see you inside the door,' and then disappears.

For a moment we stand there, dazed.

Then I take Peter's hand, pull him up the stairs and knock at the door on the second floor bearing the name-plate 'Hilde Busch'. Our stepmother comes and opens the door, and immediately hugs Peter; leading him into the kitchen, she seems happy; I follow lamely behind. 'How did this little rascal behave?' she asks, looking only at him.

Peter rouses from his torpor and pipes up, 'I saw the Führer and the buckle!'

'What buckle?' Ursula inquires.

'The Führer said he was going to give me his buckle!' Peter declares.

'That's not true!' I say. 'He didn't really say that!'

'Yes, he did!' he insists, and kicks the air.

'So what's the truth?' our stepmother asks, and looks at me.

'The Führer said,' I reply calmly, 'that at the end of the war Peter could have a buckle like his, that's what he said!'

'That's not true!' shrieks Peter.

'Marianne said a real German never lies,' I remind him, looking at him reproachfully. But his mouth starts quivering, and Ursula leaps to his aid. 'It's all right, we believe you, my love,' and she hugs him again. I feel superfluous.

Opa appears, attracted by the noise, his blanket thrown over his shoulders. 'Here you are at last!' he exclaims, and waves his pipe about, smiling contentedly. He immediately notices the plaster on my calf and asks with concern, 'My goodness, what has happened to you, Helga?'

Our stepmother echoes her father: 'Goodness, what have you done to yourself?' She seems a little embarrassed not to have noticed the plaster before. I tell them about the raid, about the doorway where we took shelter, the injured boy, the tooth I lost and my fear of losing Peter. Opa checks my leg and says, 'Maybe you should see a doctor.'

'Oh absolutely, there are gangs of doctors roaming around out there!' Ursula says sarcastically. I try to reassure Opa, telling him it's nothing but a graze, and I realise that I'm imitating Marianne's rough, masculine manners. I finish by saying that the driver disinfected the wound properly and that if I don't develop a fever I'll be fine in a couple of days. Opa calms down and looks at me with his kindly, intelligent eyes; I convince myself that he loves me a little and nearly weep with gratitude.

Then Opa says he has managed to find some dry sliced bread and asks us if we want some. Peter announces distractedly that he isn't hungry (small wonder: he ate all his sandwiches and the marzipan as well, while I lost my packet during the air-raid!). I am hungry, and ask for some bread. Then Peter pipes up, 'I want some bread too!'

'I thought you just said you weren't hungry?' Opa asks, baffled.

'That's not true, I am hungry!' says Peter brazenly, and Opa glances meaningfully at Ursula, but she ignores him and says, 'Give him a bit of bread if he's hungry, poor thing!'

All of a sudden Hilde appears; she has evidently returned from her 'special mission', but she has a fever. She asks how the stay in the bunker went, but when she hears about the air-raid she grows agitated, goes to the phone and calls Marianne. But Marianne isn't back yet. Perhaps Hilde wants to thank her friend for everything she has done; she redials at regular intervals and is finally put through. They speak for a long time, and every now and again Hilde coughs; her voice is hoarse, and at the end of the call she comes back into the kitchen and says, looking at Peter, 'I haven't been hearing good things about you, my boy.'

'Me?' says Peter, opening his eyes wide.

'Yes, you!'

'It isn't true,' mumbles Peter, fiddling with his braces.

'Marianne said you were bossy and badly behaved,' Hilde says severely. 'She says you deserve to be punished!'

Peter scratches the end of his nose, screws up his face, glances towards the bathroom and says, 'I need a pee.' And in an instant he is gone.

When he comes back, our stepmother interrogates him: 'Is it true that you were bossy and badly behaved?'

'No.'

'That's what Marianne says.'

'No!'

'And he's a liar as well,' Hilde observes, and goes back to her room. She seems to be really annoyed.

Peter stands there sulkily, but in the end Ursula says, 'Fine, let's talk about it another time. Just for once, we don't want to know the truth.'

Peter revives in an instant and starts telling her about his meeting with the Führer. Our stepmother listens with a smile, hanging on his every word, cuddling him with her eyes, while I grow increasingly jealous. When Peter finally reaches the point when he repeats, 'I'm fine, Herr Hitler, what a lovely buckle,

94

Herr Hitler!' our stepmother bursts into a peal of high-pitched laughter, revealing that she's lost a filling. Opa smiles too. Peter can be an excellent actor when he wants to be.

Our stepmother goes on laughing, but her laughter sounds artificial here in this kitchen, with its sink where no dishes are washed because not a single drop of water comes out of the tap, and where nothing is cooked any more because there is no gas, and there are no ingredients to cook with. Peter won't stop talking about the Führer, so Opa and I move to Hilde's study.

The room is freezing, and Opa puts a blanket around my shoulders. The windows are blacked out, so we light an oil lamp. I tell Opa my version of the meeting with the Führer, I say how old and ill I found him, and how uneasy I felt. Opa observes, 'Thanks to Goebbels, people imagine that the Führer is still in the best of health. Nazi propaganda is devilishly efficient.' He coughs for a long time, and it's clear that he isn't terribly well, but all of a sudden the air-raid warning sounds, and we run to the front door. Hilde comes out of her room and exclaims, 'Not again! This can't go on!' and gets ready to go to the cellar. Opa picks up his case, and our stepmother does the same. Peter picks up his teddy bear, and together we run down the stairs, where voices and frantic footsteps echo. The usual anxious scramble.

And here it is again, the damp stench of the cellar, of unwashed bodies, urine, oil lamps. Hilde lies on a camp bed; she is shivering, very ill. Peter has curled up in a corner with Teddy under his arm. He yawns, slips on to one side and goes to sleep. Our stepmother lays him on a bunk bed. 'He must be exhausted,' she says emotionally, as though no-one else might be exhausted. The others ask me about our 'holiday' in the Führer's bunker; I detect a hint of spite in their questions. But all at once the cacophony strikes up again. First an intense rumble, then a violent explosion followed by others in quick succession. The shelter shakes. Peter wakes up and shouts, 'I want Marianne!'

My utter exhaustion almost manages to block out the terror of the bombs. Opa says, 'Lie down, my little one, and forget everything if you can.' And he helps me to climb on to the bunk above Peter's. I try not to think of the planes out there, with their cargo of death and destruction, and concentrate instead on the wall. It smells unpleasantly of mould. There is a water pipe through which nothing has flowed for some time, and an enormous cobweb stretches in the corner.

The mood is tense, and the oil lamp casts flickering, ghostly shadows on the walls. The cellar is packed full, we are all crammed in on top of one another. A little girl sobs, an old man whimpers. Another curses. Faces are haggard with bottomless anxiety, there is a quiescent despair in those bodies racked with hunger, deprivation and lack of sleep. Nothing but husks, their muscles weak and their faces hollow, mere shadows of human beings.

After one particularly deafening explosion, a baby begins to wail, its howls of protest piercing us to the marrow.

'Our Father, who art in heaven . . .' Old Frau Fichtner resumes her litany, and everyone glares at her. Frau Fichtner is a widow, and two of her grandsons are missing in Russia. Her face is ashen, and her hands are criss-crossed with a spider's web of veins. 'Lord, grant that the Wenck Army may repel the enemy and restore our peace. Hail Mary . . . the fruit of thy womb, Jesus . . .'

'You can stop that right now!' Frau Köhler shouts menacingly and plants herself in front of Frau Fichtner. The old woman is dumbstruck for a moment, and, with her rosary wrapped around her fingers, she stares at the other woman with an expression of stubborn defiance and goes on praying.

'Stop it!' Frau Köhler is livid. There is a long burst of artillery fire, and Frau Fichtner shouts, 'Our Father, who art in heaven . . .'

'Enough!' Frau Köhler hurls herself at Frau Fichtner, pressing a hand over her mouth. The old woman pants and rolls her eyes. No-one intervenes, and the raid continues outside. But the moment Frau Köhler takes her hand away, the other woman goes on imperturbably, even more fervently than before: 'Hail Holy Queen, mother of mercy . . .' Old Köhler's hands press around old Fichtner's neck, which turns purple and throbs violently. I worry that she is about to die, but fortunately she recovers. With a wheezing sigh she adjusts the folds of her taffeta dress and starts praying again. Frau Köhler shakes her head and goes for a walk in the corridor to cool down. When she comes back, she tries to ignore Frau Fichtner.

During an interval of relative calm, an old man

announces with timid urgency, 'I need the toilet.'

The concierge snaps, 'There's a bucket in the corridor!'

'Could someone take me there . . . please,' he begs.

The concierge's index finger drills an imaginary hole between the old man's eyes. 'You can go to the corridor like everyone else!'

'But I'm frightened,' he protests in a querulous voice.

'We're all frightened here, for heaven's sake!' the woman yells in exasperation, 'but we all go to the bucket, even the children!'

'I can't make it that far . . .' whines the poor man.

At that point Frau Köhler asks sarcastically, 'So why don't you hang yourself?'

Then a slim little fair-haired girl gets up, goes to the corridor, comes back with the bucket and puts it at the old man's feet. Pressing one hand to his fly, he gives her a look of boundless gratitude, then gets to his feet, picks up the bucket, slips off into a corner and urinates with a series of embarrassing splashes. The concierge observes with needless mockery, 'There you are, take a good look, the epitome of the German *Übermensch*, could there be a more edifying spectacle?' And she laughs cruelly. But all of a sudden a deafening rumble thunders right over our heads. That's it, they've hit the building, I think with terror, waiting for the ceiling to collapse, but it doesn't happen. However, our lamp starts behaving erratically. The flame swoops, leaps and darts frantically, casts one last ragged shadow on the wall and expires. There are cries of panic. Someone lights a torch, examines the lamp and observes, 'Ladies and gentlemen, we are out of oil. From now on, we will have to make do with tallow candles.'

'Tallow candles!' someone groans.

'Tallow candles irritate my eyes!' Herr Hammer complains.

'And do you have any other suggestions?' snarls a woman with a face so emaciated it looks like a skull. Herr Hammer hunches his shoulders and snorts.

I gradually become acquainted with the people who come to the cellar. There are the Heinzes, man and wife, who never say a word. They sit in a corner clinging to one another, hardly involving themselves in the problems of the others. Frau Heinze suffers from depression. The little girl who brought the bucket to the old man is called Erika. She has tuberculosis. Herr Hammer is an irascible fellow who has changed his ways. A former admirer of Hitler, he now curses him from the cellar's dark corners.

One evening, in an unusually irritable mood, Herr Hammer starts a fight with Opa. 'Well, here we are with our tallow candle, and what about the Nazis' cellar? I expect they've got emergency generators! Why haven't we got an emergency generator?'

Opa looks at him uncomprehendingly. 'Goodness, Herr Hammer, I . . .'

'Surely you could arrange to have a generator installed, Herr Busch, when your daughter works for such an important Ministry!'

'Your insinuations are entirely gratuitous,' Opa replies calmly.

'Not a bit of it!' says Herr Hammer aggressively. 'And I'll tell you something else, Herr Busch, whether you like it or not. I find it hard to believe that anyone apart from people with Party membership cards can have their grandchildren fattened up in the bunker of the Reich Chancellery!'

Opa is about to reply, but Hilde intervenes: 'No-one in my family has a Party membership card, Herr Hammer, let that be clear once and for all!'

But Herr Hammer explodes into malicious laughter. 'Yes, of course! And more to the point, no-one works with Goebbels! Who do you take me for, Fräulein Busch? I'm not a complete idiot!' The others show little interest in his diatribe; every now and again Herr Hammer's arteriosclerosis gets the better of him.

But Frau Köhler, the concierge, throws oil on the flames: 'That's right, why do we not have electric light, Fräulein Busch? I was wondering that as well. Do show a little interest, come on now!'

Hilde defends herself, perplexed. 'I wouldn't have expected that of you, Frau Köhler!'

'Then why can't I send my Rudolf to the Führer's bunker, Fräulein Busch?' urges Frau Köhler pointedly.

Maintaining her composure, Hilde replies, 'Why don't you send in an application, Frau Köhler?'

Frau Köhler replies with a malevolent chuckle, 'Tell me seriously, Fräulein Busch, or do you take me for a fool?'

My stepmother intervenes: 'Don't get involved, Hilde, you're still unwell.'

The dispute comes to an end when Erika is racked

by a coughing fit and Frau Köhler goes to tend to her. She is half-angel and half-demon, it occurs to me. A very odd character.

One evening Erika and her mother, refugees from the eastern provinces, had turned up at the cellar asking for help. They had brought only a suitcase containing a few valuables, including an old family soup tureen that had proved useful in light of Erika's condition. Frau Köhler had not had the heart to send them away, not least because of the precarious state of Erika's health.

'TB – that's all we need!' grumbles one of the old men. 'That girl should be in an infectious diseases ward! Everyone risks being infected, I've said it a hundred times!' And he looks askance at the poor girl, who is busy coughing her lungs up.

Her mother's face twitches almost imperceptibly. Finally she replies, mortified, 'No-one's willing to take her in.'

'So we're all going to end up with TB,' the man replies meanly.

Then Frau Köhler explodes: 'I'm fed up to the back teeth with you, you old wreck! You might bear in mind that tuberculosis only attacks young tissue, not a decrepit old man's! So stop getting in such a state.'

'I'm only fifty-nine!' croaks the old man.

'Well if you're only fifty-nine, my dear sir, you're wearing it incredibly badly!' declares Frau Köhler pointedly, looking the man up and down with disdain.

'You have the delicacy of an elephant,' he remarks, offended, and withdraws to his mattress. But at that moment the air-raid warning sounds, and two minutes later we hear the furious pounding of gunfire. Some lime rattles down the water pipe; the walls shake.

The baby resumes its wails of protest, and Frau Fichtner, wrapped in black taffeta, shouts, 'Could someone put a cork in that awful little monster's mouth! As if we didn't already have enough noise in here!'

'Well spoken!' Herr Hammer exclaims ironically, clapping his hands together. 'Well spoken, our church-going friend! Is that an example of your charity and tolerance, Frau Fichtner?' And he spits contemptuously on the ground. The baby's mother, a shy and introverted young woman, looks around dejectedly. The mournful whine of a 'Stalin organ' heralds the familiar crash. I lean over Peter's bed and see him sitting there with Teddy under his arm and his eyes wide open. He is wearing an expression of stubborn disbelief. As the mortar deafens us, Peter bows his head and clenches his fists in a terribly poignant gesture.

X

Berlin, New Year, 1945

Hunger, thirst, cold, terror, insomnia, dirt, weakness, apathy, a sense of abandonment and powerlessness: those were the ingredients of our lives spent day and night in the cellar.

One day Opa heard that there was still some food in a warehouse near Anhalter station, so he and two women from our cellar, along with a woman and an old man from another block, decided to investigate. Our stepmother didn't want Opa to expose himself to any danger, but he wouldn't listen.

They set out early in the morning, and we worried about them all day. There had been a number of air-raids, and we were afraid they mightn't come back. Just before blackout, they returned with their booty. The food was shared out among everyone in the cellar; there was a little party. Later Opa told us how things had gone.

In order to reach the warehouse, they had first had to clamber over a pile of rubble, but because it was snowing it was slippery, and Opa had sprained his ankle. Then the old man from the other block, who was armed, had forced a double iron door; all of a sudden they had found themselves face to face with a man who'd had a submachine-gun trained on them. Before he'd had a chance to fire, the old man had killed him. So that was what things had come to, killing people for a bite to eat! Opa, once a law-abiding man, now spoke about murder quite naturally.

People returning to the cellar from outside started bringing bad news about the barbaric behaviour of the Soviet troops. Women who had fled from the eastern zones told terrible stories of rapes committed by the soldiers. Meanwhile Goebbels had unleashed fierce anti-Soviet propaganda, calling the Russians primitive rapists. That increased the level of terror, especially in women with adolescent daughters. In our cellar there were Erika and Gudrun. Erika was fourteen, Gudrun almost sixteen. Gudrun had two brothers in the cellar, Egon, the same age as Peter, and Kurt, almost seventeen. There were two other little girls among us, and also a number of relatively young women.

The population of Berlin was exhausted and prepared for imminent disaster, but from the public loudspeakers Goebbels continued to rant about a phantom Wenck Army that would bring freedom and victory to the city. Some deluded souls still clung to his lies. Then rumours began circulating that the Russians had reached the Brandenburg Gate, and people started to build barricades and dig anti-personnel trenches in the streets, even though it was all a bit premature.

In this confused climate there was little sign of Hilde; often she stayed in the Chancellery bunker, but I had a sense that her privileged era at the Ministry was coming to an end.

Time passed with gruelling monotony. One day I happened to look in a mirror; I was startled by what I saw. A gaunt face, greyish-yellow skin, dark eyes: how dreadful! Filthy locks of hair were plastered to my skull, and I had such pathetic shadows under my eyes that a wave of self-hatred washed over me. I wondered with horror: Is that me? I agreed with my stepmother: how could you love such a hideous person? She loved only Peter who, despite all our privations, still had his sullen cherub's face. I tried to console myself: the others weren't such great beauties either! That very same stepmother was reduced to skin and bones, and her hair, once ash-blonde, had assumed the indefinable colour of dust. Hilde, already thin before, had been left with yellow skin after her mysterious fever.

Erika, the girl with tuberculosis, was so frail and transparent that every time she went to sleep I worried that she wouldn't wake up again, and Frau Mannheim, the elderly wife of the journalist Herr Mannheim, had such a gaunt face that it looked as though her bones had wasted away along with her muscles. Opa had finally become so emaciated that he seemed made of air. His fingers were long and white like those of a corpse, and his clothes appeared to be holding him up. He suffered from a dry, hacking cough, but of course we had no medicine to treat him. One day I saw him lying on a chair with such a desolate expression on his face that I thought he must be dead. With my heart in my mouth I gave him a good shake, and when he opened his eyes I felt such relief that I burst into tears.

Sometimes Opa checked to see how much I had forgotten of what I had learned at Eden. He checked my spelling and my multiplication tables: I loved that. But he tired quickly and was not as strict as I would have wished. I was also afraid he would reach the conclusion that it was all pointless, that we were all going to die anyway.

I was worried about Peter, too. In the past, his liveliness and his overbearing behaviour had been, in a sense, a comfort to me. As long as he could still be cocky – I thought – there was no reason to be too downcast. But even Peter's spirits had collapsed all of a sudden. During our stay in the Chancellery bunker, he had perked up and shown an indomitable spirit of rebellion, but now it was as though something within him had been extinguished. I couldn't bear it!

One day I put him to the test. I brought up the old story about the lioness in my father's painting just to provoke him. But he nodded apathetically, telling me I was right. He hadn't even the strength to contradict me! It grieved me terribly. Still, whenever he could, he used Ursula's unconditional love as a shield.

One day – I don't even know how he did it, since the cellar was never deserted – he stole a piece of bread from our meagre stores, and when the theft was discovered he had no hesitation in accusing me, even maintaining that I had already confessed to him. Our stepmother immediately dragged me into the corridor to punish me, but Opa, who had followed us, stopped her. They went and talked for a long time at the top of the stairs, and, when she came back down, she gave me a look I couldn't interpret. Finally Opa called me to the top of the stairs as well. His face, faintly lit by the electric torch, wore an expression of impotent tenderness; he looked at me for a long time and finally asked with a sigh, 'Who took the bread, Helga?'

I was embarrassed. I didn't want to betray my brother.

'You must tell the truth,' said Opa, 'whatever it is.'

I remained silent. Then he smiled 'That's fine,' he agreed. 'Let's leave it at that.'

From that moment our relationship was strengthened.

XI

Berlin, February 1945

We lived like moles in the cellar, numb and drained by
inactivity. We waited. Our minds grew dull. Sometimes we behaved like animals.

One day Egon was gnawing on a miserable stump
of bread his mother had given him. He was sitting on
a stool, holding the bread in both hands, and the
grinding of his teeth became so insistent that I became
absurdly annoyed. Then a strange thing happened.
My brother, who had been curled up in a corner with
Teddy, worryingly downcast and apathetic as usual,
suddenly leapt to his feet and jumped on Egon to take
the bread from him. Something bestial was unleashed
within me. Rather than separate the two of them, I
joined the fray. It was as though my mind had blocked
out everything apart from the absolute need to get
hold of that piece of bread. As though hypnotised, I
laid into those two little boys and, when I finally
pulled the bread from Egon's fist, dashed upstairs as
though the Devil was after me. I reached the first
landing and stopped, panting. No-one was following
me, it was silent. Everything was covered in dust,

and the windows had been shattered. I continued climbing to the top of the house, where I stopped, out of breath.

Crouching in a low, gaping window, I devoured the bread, gnawing at it like a ravenous rodent.

After swallowing the last crumb, I felt as though I was waking from a horrible dream. Only then did I realise what I had done. I was so upset that I started crying, not with remorse but with profound anxiety. Hunger had turned me into an animal! It was atrocious, inconceivable. Appalled at myself, I looked out through the little window and saw the city in flames. The spent pyre had left a vast pall of scarlet smoke over the city. It was a terrible spectacle, chilling and ghostly. I was dumbfounded.

I heard footsteps and held my breath. Finally Opa's white head appeared over the final step, and I felt my heart plummet. 'Everything's all right, little one,' he said, and I hugged him with relief.

When we went back down to the cellar, everyone stared at us. Opa told them, 'Let's forget that little incident. Helga isn't to blame. In fact, if we want to talk about blame, the man who deprived us all of our dignity is surely Adolf Hitler.'

No-one said anything, though someone cleared his throat noisily. As for me, I wanted to apologise to Peter and Egon. Egon had been given another piece of bread, which he clutched in his hands. When I murmured, 'I'm sorry, I didn't mean . . .', he gave me half of it. My heart broke.

As we sat there, slightly embarassed, the air-raid warning sounded. Bombs were falling almost constantly around this time, so hearing the sirens seemed almost more normal than not hearing them. Everyone returned to their favourite place; if we were going to die, at least it would happen where we felt most comfortable! All of a sudden I heard a crash so close that I was afraid our building had been hit. Frau Fichtner prayed nineteen to the dozen, Herr Hammer cursed Hitler, Peter clenched his fists and sat completely still, and the old people wept. Once the attack was over, someone went up to check; when he came down again, he reported that part of the top storey had been blown to pieces, but that everything else was unharmed. The two widowers who lived on that floor had to resign themselves to living in the cellar for the foreseeable future.

There was a discreet bush telegraph between the cellars in our district. Strange rumours were circulating about the Führer: there was a theory, for example, that he had escaped abroad or barricaded himself into one of his fifteen headquarters to await the end of the war. And in fact the rumours were not entirely unjustified. The last time the German people had heard the Führer's voice had been at the end of January, on the twelfth anniversary of his ascent to power; no-one had seen him in public since then, and only those who visited the Chancellery bunker could have stated definitely that he was in Berlin. We now know that until the very last moment the bunker was kept supplied with large reserves of food, while the populace, especially the people of Berlin, was literally dying of hunger. However, if anyone dared to point this out to the Führer, he flew into an incandescent rage. We also know that, although the German Army was stretched to its absolute limit, Hitler continued to insist that the troops launch pointless attacks, and anyone who refused to obey orders faced execution. Considerable numbers of soldiers could be seen hanging from the city's trees or lamp-posts, making the backdrop of Berlin even more ghostly than it was already.

Hilde went on working at the Propaganda Ministry and, when she did not stay over at the Chancellery bunker, I heard her whispering at night with Opa and my stepmother. Sometimes I recognised contradictions in the things she said. One day, for example, one of the old men in the cellar became inconsolable. He wept, he chewed his fingers, he groaned, 'I'm frightened, we're lost, the Russians are coming to kill us!' Hilde consoled him, reassuring him that the Wenck Army was definitely on its way. The old man believed her; in reality, the previous night I had heard Hilde saying that the Wenck Army was on the brink of collapse and that Berlin was irremediably lost.

In the meantime, a number of things had changed in our cellar. Most importantly, we had lost Herr and Frau Heinze. They had shot themselves after receiving the news that their only son had fallen on the Eastern front.

Frau Fichtner had recovered from a minor heart attack, and because she had done so without any medical intervention, she attributed her salvation to the Madonna. From then on she prayed day and night without drawing breath.

Frau Köhler, a true Berliner who spoke in heavy dialect when annoyed, yielded more and more to dangerous reflections on the Führer, especially since her twelve-year-old son Rudolf had taken it into his head that he wanted to join the Werewolves. This was the name given to Hitler's final initiative, developed along with Goebbels, to oppose the enemy's advance. The organisation recruited patriotic old people, women and children for a clandestine struggle as improbable as it was absurd. Frau Köhler had had no hesitation in giving her son two resounding slaps, swearing that she would lock him in the cellar till the end of the war rather than serve him up to Hitler on a silver platter for a cause that was as good as lost. She was really furious, and whenever the Führer's name was mentioned she lost her temper. Her outbursts could have been fatal if they had reached the ears of a fanatical Nazi, who would certainly have denounced her to the Gestapo.

Early one morning someone knocked at the cellar door. I awoke with my heart in my mouth. Everyone sat up in their beds, terrified. Frau Fichtner, wearing her taffeta dress, her coat and a moth-eaten mink stole, immediately began to pray. Erika tried to stifle a sudden fit of coughing. The old people wept in silence. Ursula dashed over to Peter's bed. Finally Frau Köhler went and opened the door.

Two SS men came charging down the stairs, shouting in clipped military voices, 'Everyone face the wall, children included!' And they gestured with their submachine-guns.

I thought I wouldn't manage to get out of bed. Nonetheless, we all got up; but the room was not big enough for everyone, so some people had to stand against the corridor walls, beneath the water pipes.

Standing beside me, Opa murmured, 'Don't worry, it's just a formality.' His face was terrifyingly white, and a thin blue vein throbbed in his forehead. Out of the corner of my eye I saw Peter clutching our step-mother's legs. I felt a slimy, paralysing, humiliating fear. Fear and a sense of injustice: we were children, we were innocent!

The SS men searched us roughly, sparing only the baby in its mother's arms.

All of a sudden it occurred to me that there were weapons hidden in the cellar. I knew this was a crime punishable by execution

I prayed that the SS men would not find the weapons, but they weren't even looking for them. After checking our papers, they sent us back to our places, apart from Herr Schacht.

'You're coming with us!' one of the SS men shouted to him.

He stammered, 'But what have I done?'

'Shut up, bloody Jew,' the SS man snapped.

Herr Schacht grew very agitated, wrung his hands, tried frantically to convince the SS men. 'There must be some mistake . . . my name is Schacht, I'm not a Jew . . .'

'Shut your trap!' said the other SS man, striking him in the stomach with the butt of his submachine-gun.

The poor man bent double with pain, sobbing like a child.

'Who's in charge of this building?' one of the SS men shouted. Frau Köhler stepped forward.

'Why is this Jew in this cellar?'

Confused, Frau Köhler said nothing.

'Answer!' said the SS man, aiming the machine-gun at her stomach.

Then she told him, her voice breaking with terror, that some days previously Herr Schacht had knocked at the door asking for help. He had been injured, he had had a fever, and she had taken pity on him.

They interrogated her for a long time, gave the other adults the third degree as well, and finally ordered Herr Schacht out of the cellar, pushing him towards the stairs with their guns pointed at the back of his neck. In two seconds they were gone.

We were rooted to the spot. After a long silence Frau Köhler said, 'If he really is Jewish, God help him.'

Herr Hammer observed, with a hint of optimism, 'They might have made a mistake,' but Frau Köhler spat on the dusty floor: 'They never make mistakes, and you know it!'

On another morning we were awakened by the shrieks of the concierge. 'There are heads and legs among my cabbages!' she yelled agitatedly. Severed heads, hands and guts among my cabbages!' In the autumn Frau Köhler had planted some cabbages in the courtyard, covering them with canvas to keep them from prying eyes. The previous night, someone had come into the courtyard to steal them and had been blown to pieces in the process.

'They must have been two women,' groaned Frau Köhler, and ran off to vomit.

The women's remains had to be dealt with. Frau Köhler phoned the squads responsible for the disposal of corpses but was told that there was no longer anyone available, because all the men had been sent to the front or made to join some special division or other. What was to be done with the remains of the two women, asked Frau Köhler; could they perhaps be buried in the courtyard? No! That was forbidden! Absolutely forbidden! Berlin's courtyards could not be turned into makeshift cemeteries! So she and Herr Mannheim, the only ones brave enough to do it, reassembled the women's bodies as best they could, near the shed. Not inside, because that was where the tools were kept, and there was still a chance that we might be able to use them.

But that was not the only incredible event on that chilly morning. About half an hour after the discovery of the shredded bodies among the cabbages, the young mother in our cellar noticed that her child had stopped breathing. She stroked his cold face, shook him, called to him in a voice at first anxious, then terrified and finally imploring. But it was no use: her child was dead. Frozen, I watched her horrorstruck grief, her incredulous despair. That baby, whom Frau Fichtner had called 'a little monster' for rebelling against a world that denied him his rest, had tiptoed away without disturbing anyone.

The young mother sat mutely with her child in her

arms for a day and a night, locked in her torment. The following morning, immediately after the all-clear, she got up, went to the courtyard, buried the child under a lilac bush and went up to her flat. After a while, when she did not come back, people went to look for her. They found her hanging in her bathroom.

I was profoundly upset that morning: I couldn't understand, I didn't want to understand! Feeling a surge of disgust in my belly, I ran to the bucket.

After throwing up, I stood there, exhausted and revolted, in the cold, foul-smelling corridor. All of a sudden I noticed a rat watching me. It was a repugnant animal, fat and paunchy. It stared at me with red, attentive eyes, two red-hot pins that hypnotised me. I sensed that it was about to jump at me, so I tried to scream, but the sound died in my chest like a crazed echo. I gave the bucket a kick, and it clanked dully against the wall. Then I fainted.

When I came to, I found myself in the cellar with the others, with Opa pinching my cheeks. He gave me a glass containing a finger of water, the most that would be given to any poor wretch recovering after a sudden illness. I looked over at my stepmother, but she, of course, was whispering to Peter.

XII

Water, water, we dreamed of water. As soon as it was
fetched, the precious fluid was gone. We yearned to
get drunk on it, to absorb it through our pores, to feel
quenched and cleansed.

Our thirst could not be assuaged, there were too
many of us. Although the cans didn't hold much
water, twice a week each of us was allowed an extra
ration for the purposes of personal hygiene, just
enough to perform the most basic ablutions. On top
of that there was the problem of sanitation, and the
bed-linen had to be washed! And if thirst was Hell, a
red-hot tunnel of longing, making us dream of
gushing taps and brimming fountains, hunger was just
as bad.

And then sleep, sleep; I longed to sleep for a month,
perhaps forever. But we lived from one air-raid
warning to the next, and in the rare intervals of peace,
especially at night, we had to endure the noises
everyone else made: the rattling snores of one of the
old men, the monotonous muttering of Frau Fichtner,
Erika's incessant coughing, the sneezes of Herr
Hammer with his permanent cold, the excited dis-
cussions of the Mannheims, not to mention more

embarrassing sounds. On top of this were the irritating creaks of the rudimentary bunk beds and the squeaks of the camp beds on which Egon, Kurt and Gudrun slept.

One morning we woke up with strange red lumps on our bodies. We soon realised that our shelter was infested with bed-bugs.

We began a furious campaign against those foul creatures by checking every centimetre of our beds, because we had no chemical means of eliminating them. I discovered a few in my mattress and felt very ashamed; I was afraid I might be particularly dirty, but of course that wasn't the case. We were all just as dirty as each other! Soon, in fact, we found bed-bugs in almost all the mattresses, and we had no option but to throw them into the courtyard; after which we went up to our own flats and reluctantly brought down our good mattresses, which also took up more space. Yet another problem in our cramped cellar!

Everyone tried to make the time pass as best they could. Someone, in the flickering candle-light, flicked back and forth through an old photograph album; Herr Hammer admired and re-admired his collection of butterflies caught on trips to the remote countryside or in the meadow behind his birthplace, a little village in Bavaria. Frau Bittner knitted socks for the soldiers at the front, knowing full well that her efforts were pointless. Apart from anything else, she wouldn't have known where to send them; and besides, at that stage in the war there were plenty of things the Army needed more than rough woollen socks. Rudolf endlessly reread the adventures of Karl May, books warmly recommended by the Nazi regime.

Peter no longer talked about the Führer, and had become so strange and taciturn that I barely recognised him. When Opa tried to distract him by offering to tell him a fairy-tale, he always refused apathetically, saying he would rather sleep. But the quietest and shyest of all was Gudrun, who had just had her sixteenth birthday, of course without a party or a present. She had scornfully rejected the socks knitted by her mother. Gudrun spent hour after hour crouching in a corner, staring blankly at the table with the suitcases stowed beneath it, and growing animated only when her brother Egon irritated her by teasing her about her breasts. These had appeared, round and conspicuous, in the course of a week, a phenomenon that both startled and annoyed her.

Since leaving Eden, I had acquired a collection of new fears which I classified according to their importance. First on the list was the fear of bombs, a fear you don't get used to. The melancholy whistle of the 'Stalin organs' always made me shudder. Besides, each air-raid seemed determined to confirm the world's absolute enmity towards me, and I continued to wonder what crime I had committed to deserve it.

Second was the terrified thought that we would not be able to scrape together enough to eat, not even turnips or rotten potatoes or mouldy bread. I imagined dying in the cellar despite Herr Hammer's assurances that death by starvation would not be painful.

I was also troubled by the fear that the public pumps would stop giving water, and that we would all die of thirst.

In fact, if those fears had not been uppermost in my mind, linked as they were to my most basic needs, my greatest terror would have been the thought of losing Opa. When he coughed till he turned blue, I was always afraid he might suffocate; and when he went out to get water, I prayed the shells would spare him. Sometimes I ventured beyond the hope that he would not die, and wished that he would stay with me even in the future, and see me grow up.

I always tried to be nice to him. I brought him his ration of water or polished his shoes by spitting on them. This I did on my own initiative, but he said with a laugh that I must have learned it from the street urchins of Naples. He told me how those boys lived, and when I compared their life with mine, they seemed much luckier than me.

I think I always behaved correctly with Opa, but Ursula continued to complain about me. 'My God, Helga really is a trial,' she used to say to Opa. 'That child refuses to become part of our family.'

Kurt, Frau Bittner's third son, who was almost seventeen and whose beard had started growing, had from one day to the next turned into an aggressive and short-tempered boy. He was forever telling his mother that he felt useless, that he wanted to do something for the Fatherland. At this time the SS were issuing appeals from their loudspeakers and megaphones, saying that all males between the ages of fifteen and sixty could join a special unit, the City Defenders, the umpteenth bright idea they had come up with for resisting the enemy. Kurt thought of joining up, but he had not reckoned with his mother's stern resistance. Frau Bittner told him that while she was still breathing, no Nazi unit was going to slaughter her son, and ordered him not to move from the cellar until the war ended, unless it was absolutely necessary. Kurt threatened to escape, to present himself at the nearest military headquarters the moment his mother turned her back; he frightened her to death, poor woman, but in the end he stayed in the cellar, irritating everyone with his sullen rage. Among us there were also two men just under the age of sixty, who had been gripped by sudden panic. They emphatically did not want to be recruited as City Defenders and decided not to leave the cellar, not even to go and fetch water. So it was the oldest people, like Opa, and the women who had to assume the task of supplying water and food. When all was said and done, we were a small community, and solidarity was compulsory if we didn't want anyone to die of thirst or hunger. Hilde was also a great help because every now and again, when we were on the brink of starvation, she would provide us with the most basic foodstuffs. But now she had to do it secretly; it was forbidden to let so much as a pin leave the Chancellery bunker.

We received news that my father had been injured and was in a military hospital near Frankfurt. I wept with joy; at least I knew he was alive!

One day Herr Hammer returned to the cellar with half a sack of strange roots, insisting they were edible.

The fire was lit, the roots were boiled, but after eating them we all went down with dysentery. We were forced to add another two buckets at the end of the cellar corridor, and for a few days there was a real procession, made even more difficult by the fact that we had run out of toilet paper. There were only some old newspapers – by this time the daily papers were no longer being published – and we used them sparingly!

About a week after the mishap with the roots, Frau Fichtner exclaimed, just as the air-raid warning was sounding, 'My God, I've had enough of all this; why can't I just die?' She closed her eyes, rolled over on her side and died. At first we thought she was asleep, but her body looked too stiff and strange.

'A fine death,' Herr Hammer commented, 'I wouldn't mind going like that myself!'

Again the problem of how to dispose of the corpse arose. 'At least that one won't smell,' one of the old men commented acidly. 'She was too pious for that.'

'You should be ashamed,' Frau Köhler said reproachfully. 'Idleness has sharpened your tongue. You'd be better off going to fetch the water from time to time.'

'I have a heart condition,' the man whined. 'I mustn't exert myself.'

'Well, you give your tongue plenty of exercise,' Frau Köhler replied curtly. 'Down here there's no shortage of excuses for not fetching water!'

The old man began to cry.

'A true German never cries, didn't anyone teach you that at school?' asked Frau Köhler spitefully.

'I have a heart condition . . .' the old man repeated, like a stuck record.

'Then shut your trap,' Frau Köhler snapped back. Frau Fichtner must be buried in the courtyard, peace be on her soul.' And that was what happened. She was placed beside the remains of the two bodies blasted apart among the cabbages, and the whole lot covered over with a tarpaulin.

One day I followed Opa as he left the cellar to fetch water. I walked behind him like a little dog following the only source of warmth that existed in the world; the others thought I was going to the bucket.

When I found myself in the street, I saw him turn the corner and went on following him. All of a sudden I found myself facing a barrier of burning buildings; I was immediately overwhelmed by a wave of heat and that intense burning smell that takes your breath away and lingers on your clothes for a long time. I kept to the centre of the road to avoid collapsing walls. The air was black with smoke, so, afraid of losing sight of Opa, I started to run. I slipped in the snow, and my shoes were soaked, becoming frozen and heavy. I kept going through the smoke. I passed a Volkswagen, crumpled and covered with dust. Inside it a decomposing corpse still sat at the wheel.

I went on running along the street, which was scattered with obstacles: rusted motorcycles, twisted bicycles, a little van bearing the inscription *Emmerhasen Butchers*, a toilet, bed-frames, the remains of an abandoned barricade. I reached a square where almost all of the houses had been flattened by bombs. Four tree-lined streets branched off it. The trees were bare and charred, as though they had been drenched in paraffin. Some signs of the square's former loveliness remained: Baroque lanterns hanging twisted and ruined, misshapen iron benches, shattered footpaths. On an advertising pillar the familiar Nazi slogans incited hatred. The place was terribly sad and desolate. A large rat crossed the road, followed by its young. Even the rats had families!

Seeing that Opa had stopped, I also did. He was studying what remained of a row of elegant shops, now reduced to wretched black caves in which the wind played, stirring the vast, delicate cobwebs.

All of a sudden I heard a distant rumble, coming closer quickly, too quickly! Air-raids increasingly happened without warning. Panicking, I saw Opa start to run. At the same time a hail of artillery-fire passed over my head, striking the balcony of a bombed building, which crashed to the ground. Crazed with fear, I started running too, joining Opa, who had taken refuge in a doorway. When I tugged on his coat, he looked down and exclaimed in consternation: 'My God! What on earth are you doing here?' And he hugged me to him while the street was swept by shells.

The air was thick with dust, and a hail of rubble fell on us. I thought I was going to suffocate. My mouth and nostrils filled with dust, and I began to cough so violently that I couldn't breathe. Opa slapped me repeatedly on the back, shouting, 'Breathe, Helga, please breathe, my darling!' When I caught my breath, I saw Opa sobbing with relief.

Finally, when the planes had moved on, Opa gripped my hand and we hurled ourselves out of the doorway, reaching the entrance to the U-Bahn about thirty metres away. The stairs were slippery with snow, and I slipped again, hitting my knee. But I said nothing.

The tunnel was full of people: old men, women and children, *Volkssturm* militia, ordinary soldiers, SS men. The air was dank and foul. There was the faint sound of children crying, and a woman was giving birth on the bare floor, surrounded by bewildered people.

We sat down on the tiles. A woman repeated obsessively, 'The Hohenzollerndamm has been on fire since yesterday.' She tried to attract the attention of a mother who was looking after two children. The mother pulled down the trousers of one of the two children, who arched his back and peed on the rails.

'The Hohenzollerndamm has been burning since yesterday, and I have nothing left!'

The mother turned, gripped the woman's arm in a gesture of solidarity and replied, 'I have nothing left either, no house, no husband, not even a bed for my children. The whole city is burning, and there's nothing we can do about it.'

An old woman was sitting with her back against the white tiles, knitting. Socks, I thought to myself, socks for the soldiers at the front. Above us there was a relentless commotion, then we heard the impact of the umpteenth 'Stalin organ'. 'The *U-Bahn* is the most dangerous place you could find,' croaked an old man with an amputated arm. 'The smallest-calibre weapon could penetrate it.'

Opa murmured a joke in my ear, 'As you can see, we're in the right place. When this performance is over, we'll make a run for it,' he added.

No sooner had the all-clear howled than we rushed for the entrance, but once we were outside we were struck by the stench of burning, and, next to the entrance, we ran into a tangle of corpses, a confusion of chopped meat, bleeding flesh. Opa dragged me away, saying, 'Don't look, my child, that's enough, don't look!' We crossed the square. 'I'm thirsty,' I said. A terrible thirst stuck my tongue to the roof of my mouth. 'When we get to the pump, you'll be able to drink,' Opa promised me. We immediately hit a road block. 'Halt! Stop!' A group of young SS men aimed their submachine-guns at us. 'Where are you going?'

Opa gestured to the cans with his chin. 'To get some water.'

'Papers!'

Opa put down the cans and took his papers out of his coat pocket. One of the SS men checked them carefully; although they were combing the city in search of people to enrol in various improvised units, Opa was too old to be eligible. 'All in order!' one of the SS men shouted finally, nodding to us to go on our way.

Beneath a twisted traffic-light that hadn't worked for ages, Opa said, 'You shouldn't have followed me, Helga. Why did you?'

He was trying to look severe in his crumpled coat.

'I just wanted to be with you . . .' I murmured uncertainly.

His eyes lingered on my face for a moment, then his expression softened. 'Fine,' he said benignly. 'I'll have a word with your stepmother.' And he picked up the cans.

I was starting to feel tired, but by now we were close to the pump. There was a long queue consisting chiefly of women, their feet in the slush, their faces tense and their eyes veiled with infinite weariness. We took our places. 'I'm thirsty,' I repeated, but Opa replied, 'You'll have to wait, my child, I'm really sorry.'

After a while an old woman in front of us, toothless and dressed in rags, started to rant and rave. She raged against Hitler, the war and the regime, using terms so offensive that another woman felt obliged to warn her that someone might hear her and denounce her to the Gestapo. But she persisted, brandishing an enamel pot. 'Let them arrest me, what possible difference could it make to me now?'

We waited a long time for our turn, and in the end I couldn't feel my feet. They were like two blocks of ice.

Finally it was my turn, and I threw myself blindly forward to drink; I caught as much water as I could in the hollow of my hands, but the others immediately started muttering. I stopped timidly, and Opa started refilling the cans; but the water came out slowly, so it took a very long time.

We set off back to the cellar. Such a long way and so much trouble for two cans of water!

We walked slowly, because the cans were heavy. I saw Opa's face screwing up with the effort and would have liked to have helped him. Every now and again he stopped, sighed and gazed up at the sky. I felt terribly sorry for him.

All of a sudden the sirens wailed again, and Opa exclaimed, 'God almighty, not another one!' He looked around for an air-raid shelter, but there were none nearby, so we slipped into the doorway of a church.

A freezing draught blasted the wide nave, and a flock of birds had just flown up through a gaping hole in the dome. The font lay in pieces on the floor, and a trunkless Christ dangled above a bare and battered altar. I saw corpses lined up against a wall and shuddered: I had had enough of corpses!

Furious gunfire had broken out outside and echoed grimly around the nave. I needed to pee. Feeling embarrassed and rather guilty, I told Opa, who replied, 'Just go ahead, my little one, don't worry about it.' So I squatted down among the pews, which still smelled of incense, and relieved myself. As I was standing up, a tremendous whine announced impending disaster: a bomb plunged into the church through one of the big windows, crashing into the opposite wall and knocking off a stucco cornice. The glass shattered with a clean, deafening noise, and splinters rained down on us. I could feel them in my hair, in my eyebrows and on the back of my neck as a crystalline echo rang out among the marble carvings and the indifferent plaster angels.

Opa had pushed me down on the floor, shielding me with his body.

When the inferno subsided, I opened my eyes and

saw a prayer-book under the pews. As I stretched to pick it up, I heard Opa asking, 'What have I got here on my forehead?'

I saw some blood just below his hairline. He sighed, looking dazed and bewildered. I asked him for a handkerchief, bathed his forehead with a little water from the cans, determined that the wound was superficial, and told him so with considerable relief.

'You are a brave girl,' Opa told me, and I was proud of myself. We set off for home once again.

A uniformed man lay just outside the church door, his intestines spilling from his gaping belly. 'Don't look,' whispered Opa, 'he's dead anyway, poor thing, and there's nothing to be done.'

Every now and again Opa stopped and sighed. His eyes were clear and dignified. Sweat flowed on to his eyelids, his cheekbones. His thin shoulders were bowed with exhaustion. I felt a great wave of love for him. We made our way home without any further difficulties.

The moment my stepmother saw us, she shouted, 'Where have you been, you stupid girl? Will you never stop running away?'

Opa gave a conciliatory reply: 'It's my fault, I asked her to come with me.'

Ursula was perplexed, but she didn't dare press the point, and inquired about Opa's injury.

'It's just a graze,' he replied. 'It's nothing. Helga tended to me. She's a good girl, a brave girl.' And he stroked my hair.

Peter frowned at me. 'When I'm big I want to shoot everybody. I looked for you under the stairs.'

'We were all looking for you,' added my step-mother, glancing at me with impotent rage.

'It's my fault,' Opa repeated.

'Where were you when the warning sounded?' Ursula asked.

'Which one?' asked Opa distractedly, trying to make us smile. 'The first one or the second one?'

'The second one,' she replied. 'They say that second raid was a heavy one.'

'In a church,' said Opa. 'A church full of birds and corpses. We deserve a glass of water!'

'Me too, me too!' Peter piped up, and went to fetch his glass. Everyone else in the cellar held out their own receptacles as well.

Water. Water. A thousand times more precious because we had risked our lives to get it.

XIII

Berlin, April 1945

Flu broke out in our cellar, and the fact that we were living in such close quarters encouraged the infection to spread. The place assumed an apocalyptic air: we were piled on top of one another, feverish and coughing, spreading germs all around us. Our bodies resembled husks. In the light of a smoking candle, we waited for a merciful God to free us from our sad existences.

Opa became seriously ill with asthma. He was seized by violent fits of breathlessness which worried me deeply: I was afraid he would suffocate.

Hilde managed to get hold of a supply of aspirins but then left us to avoid becoming infected herself. She didn't fall ill, but Erika did, developing a high fever and becoming so weak that her life was in danger. She was delirious, and her body shook with terrifying coughing fits.

Peter just felt vaguely unwell for a few days.

Our stepmother, on the other hand, developed an intestinal flu that forced her to walk back and forth frequently from her bed to the bucket. I fell ill too, vomiting and coughing, and my scalp was covered with ugly, suppurating scabs. Opa said this was due to the lack of vitamins. If only that had been all.

In spite of everything, we all recovered, one after the other. After surviving tons of bombs, it would have been ridiculous to die of flu!

One day, I was seized by an overwhelming desire for a breath of fresh air. I asked Ursula's permission to go out to the courtyard for a moment, but she said no. Always categorical, she never tried to understand my moods or my needs. It was really curious that Opa's daughter should be such a 'Prussian' person, when he was a man of extraordinary intuition and humanity. Perhaps she had inherited her rigidity from her mother.

Opa took his daughter aside. They had a short conversation, and in the end my stepmother allowed me five minutes in the open air.

'I'll come with you and wait in the doorway,' Opa said. I opened the little door leading to the courtyard with an intensity of emotion that took my breath away; I was dazzled by the light and had to close my eyes. When I opened them again, I saw the sun and filled my lungs, greedily breathing the spring air even if it did smell of burning and corpses.

Suddenly I saw how dirty I was, and my joy evaporated. I was ashamed of myself. Beneath the radiant sun I felt like a mole, a poor mole that had emerged for a moment from its wretched hole.

I overcame my despair and looked around me. The atmosphere was one of sinister enchantment. It was hot. The lilac bush was covered with buds that would soon burst into blossom. The sun seemed the most neutral thing in existence. It shed its light on the ugly and the beautiful, the pathetic and the solemn, vice and virtue. The sun was incorruptible. Men might be able to destroy Berlin, or perhaps the whole world, but the sun would shed light on all the horrors, and in the end it would restore some of life's warmth!

Opa waited in the doorway, warning me that I had already used up three of my five minutes, when suddenly I was filled with a feeling of rebellion. Five minutes of freedom, compared to a whole childhood spent imprisoned by the war, was a truly ridiculous privilege.

Opa studied the treacherous sky. From one moment to the next a squadron of planes might appear over the tops of those ruins, fire at us and kill us. The sun would shed its light on our torn bodies, make our blood look all the more vivid and frightening.

'You've got one more minute,' Opa warned me. Now I was getting angry. For heaven's sake, what could I accomplish in a minute?

I glanced at the concierge's cabbages, among which the two women's bodies had fallen to pieces. They wilted on their stubby stems, suffering the greedy attention of a blackbird. Some daisies grew in a patch of luxuriant grass: I was tempted to pick them but then changed my mind. I remembered some lines from a poem by Goethe, the meaning of which had been explained by the headmistress of Eden. The poem told the story of a man who, walking on a heath, had seen a beautiful flower. He had tried to pick it, but the little plant had asked him sadly, 'Are you going to pick me so that I shall wither?'

All of a sudden the wind changed, and my nostrils filled with the repugnant reek of the corpses rotting at the side of the shed; I was struck by a feeling of nausea so deep that I wanted the earth to swallow me up. I hated everything. Blinded by hatred, I ran towards the door. Opa looked at me uncomprehendingly and said, 'I was going to let you have an extra five minutes, my darling!' But I replied in a hostile, rebellious, resentful voice: 'I don't want them! I don't want your stupid five minutes! I don't want anything, I just want to die!' And back I went, quivering, to my prison.

Opa joined me in the cellar and hugged me. 'My poor child . . .' he murmured, 'my poor child . . .' Then he pulled away and said in a more practical voice, 'I'm going to have to fetch some water.'

'But it's not your turn!' I protested, and he replied that my stepmother was unwell, so he preferred to go in her place.

I saw him picking up the cans and going slowly upstairs. I felt sad and depressed. When Peter woke up I told him, 'I was out in the courtyard and saw some daisies.'

Envy revived him. 'I want to go to the courtyard as well,' he announced and jumped down from the bed. Egon, who just happened to awake at that moment, echoed him: 'I want to go to the courtyard! Me too!'

My stepmother looked at me irritably. 'Couldn't you keep your mouth shut? I knew this was going to happen!'

'So can I go?' asked Peter, standing stoutly in front of Ursula.

'No, my love.' She should never have said it. Egon

and Peter staged a little revolt, which took a considerable time to quell. Finally Peter looked at me with hate in his eyes and announced, 'I'm never going to speak to you again for the rest of my life!' I was glad he had recovered some of his old grit.

Dismissed by Peter, I withdrew into a corner and kept watch on the stairs. After a while Erika asked me to tell her about the courtyard, so I squatted down next to her and told her about the sun, the lilac buds and the green grass, but I left out the red sky and the smell of burning and of corpses. She talked about her village, its pond with two swans, gullies lined with myrtle-blossom and a river on whose banks the children told each other stories in summer. She told me the story of her escape as well; first from the Germans, and then from the terrible Russians who had nailed her grandfather to the stable door and raped her mother. We talked until she was seized by a coughing fit, at which point her mother asked me to leave her alone.

There was another air-raid warning, and the usual cacophony began. I didn't know anyone who was dead apart from Frau Fichtner, so I prayed to her to protect Opa, who was outside with the water cans.

Once the attack was over, we all looked at each other with relief: we were safe once again. Peter unclenched his fists, Gudrun loosened the jumper covering her young breasts. One of the old men was crying; he looked at us with clear, desperate eyes.

'What's wrong?' asked Frau Bittner. 'Hasn't he got used to the raids?' She went over to him and laid a friendly hand on his shoulder. Sobbing, the old man said, 'When you're all asleep I'm going to kill myself, I've got a pistol in my underpants.'

Some of us smiled in disbelief, Peter stared at the man with great interest, Herr Hammer said, 'What poppycock!' and Frau Köhler decided to make a joke of it: 'At least he's got something hard in his pants. Congratulations, my dear Herr Spitzberg!' Herr Spitzberg took offence. 'I demand respect, Frau Köhler,' he said gravely. 'I was once a celebrated actor, my Egmont met with great acclaim! I have performed in all the best theatres in the Reich, Frau Köhler, even in your Schlossparktheater, if that means anything to you!'

'Egmont!' bleated the concierge, who could be a real rascal when the occasion called for it. 'They should have cut your head off for real, Herr Spitzberg, then at least you wouldn't have to croak in this dirty old cellar!'

'I'm going to kill myself,' the old man muttered, and slipped his hand into his trousers.

'What's he doing?' teased Frau Köhler, who refused to take him seriously. 'Checking he has something hard in his knickers?' But all of a sudden Kurt came up behind Herr Spitzberg, darted his hand into the man's trouser pocket and brought out a pistol. Herr Hammer shouted, 'God almighty, Herr Spitzberg, you're insane! Who gave you permission to take the pistol from its hiding place? You know that if the Gestapo come down here and find a weapon, they'll put you up against the wall and shoot you?'

'Let them,' the old man exploded. A few seconds later he lay down on one of the camp beds and started snoring.

Herr Hammer took the gun from Kurt and said, 'Don't get any ideas, young man, that thing's going back where it came from, right this minute!'

'I want the gun!' exclaimed Rudolf, Frau Köhler's son. But his mother cuffed him around the ear: 'I'll give you guns! Has everyone gone mad around here?'

Darkness had already fallen by the time Opa came downstairs: I was immediately aware that something was wrong. With a curious stiffness in his movements, he put down the cans, raised his eyes to the ceiling for a moment and fell to the ground. My stepmother cried out while my heart started pounding. 'Please, God, let him not be dead!' I thought.

Everyone rushed over to Opa, but Herr Mannheim sent us back to our seats, imposing calm and silence. Then he removed Opa's coat, and from my bed I saw that his clothes were drenched in blood. I almost fainted.

'He's been hit,' Herr Mannheim announced. 'We must at all costs find a doctor, he's losing too much blood.' Herr Mannheim put on his coat and went out, despite his wife's protests. Frau Köhler froze the woman with a look but said nothing. No-one had any idea how to help Opa, and there was a terrible air of tension in the cellar. My stepmother held her father's hand and wept. Peter kept asking why she was crying.

Someone, perhaps to relieve the tension, said, 'You won't believe it, but this evening some lunatic's giving a concert in the Beethoven-Saal, and do you know what's on the programme?'

'A symphony for artillery and mortar-fire?' suggested Herr Hammer.

'No. Beethoven's *Egmont* overture and *Death and Transfiguration* by Strauss.'

At the word *Egmont*, Herr Spitzberg woke up as if from a spell and shouted, 'Who's playing the part of Egmont?'

'Stop shouting!' said Herr Hammer. 'They're not acting, they're playing the overture.'

'Where?' asked Herr Spitzberg, suddenly very alert.

'In the Beethoven-Saal.'

'They're giving a concert in the Beethoven-Saal?' he repeated, his face brightening. 'That means the war's over!'

'Your arse it is!' hissed Herr Hammer. 'Be quiet, though, can't you see that Herr Busch is ill?'

Footsteps were heard at the top of the steps, and Herr Mannheim appeared, supporting a decrepit old man with only one leg.

'This is Dr Schreber,' he announced. 'He is going to take care of Herr Busch.'

The doctor asked for a glass of water, took a long drink and motioned for the first-aid bag Herr Mannheim had brought for him.

Expertly extracting a long splinter of glass from Opa's spine, the doctor treated the wound, gave him a few stitches, checked that the lung was unharmed, said, 'That's done, he'll be better by tomorrow' and then slumped on to a chair and went to sleep. After a few seconds he awoke and told us, in a sprightly voice, that he had spent forty years working at the Elisabeth-Hospital in Berlin. 'Everything worked perfectly well ... I don't know how they cope now, without water or electricity or anaesthetics or medicines ... the world has gone mad ... I wish I was dead!' With that he went back to sleep. There was something unbearably gloomy about the sight of his stump in the smoky candle-light. Peter went over to the doctor, frowned and asked, 'Where's the other bit of his leg?'

Everyone told him to be quiet.

'Where's the other bit of his leg?' Peter repeated loudly. At which the doctor awoke again and replied, 'A shell took it, my boy. Could you promise me one thing?'

'Yes,' whispered Peter, embarrassed.

'Promise me that when you grow up, you won't allow another war to happen,' said the old man.

'Why?' asked Peter.

'Because war is unworthy of men.'

'Why?'

'Because in war people are forced to behave in an unnatural way.'

'Why?'

'You, for example, are always in this cellar. Does that seem right to you?'

'Yes.'

'Why does it seem right to you, my child?'

'If I go outside, I'll get killed.'

'And does it seem right to you that a little boy can't leave his house because he'll be killed if he does?'

'Well ...' Peter murmured with a shrug.

'But you'd like to go and play in the courtyard?' the doctor insisted.

'Yes,' replied Peter, 'to pick a daisy.'

'And that's all?'

'Yes. Because the courtyard stinks. There are corpses there.'

The old man murmured, 'My poor child.' His eyes were shining.

Peter rubbed his calf with the toe of his shoe and declared, 'When I'm big I want to be a bandit and kill everybody.'

'Everybody, are you sure?' asked the doctor.

Peter reflected for a moment. 'Not Mutti,' he conceded, 'and not Helga and Opa and Hilde.' He left out our father.

'Poor boy!' the doctor repeated and rose to his feet. His stump cast a monstrous shadow on the wall. 'May God protect you,' he concluded, took one last look at Opa and headed towards the stairs. Herr Mannheim offered to walk him back. At first the old man didn't want this, but finally he agreed. Frau Mannheim protested. Herr Mannheim looked at her disapprovingly: 'Please, Gitte!' When they had gone, Frau Köhler exploded, 'You are quite revoltingly selfish, Frau Mannheim!'

'My husband's always the one who volunteers,' Frau Mannheim barked back.

'We're always the ones who go and fetch water,' Frau Köhler pointed out.

'I have arthritis in my knees,' the woman moaned.

'From now on you're on the water rota,' Frau Köhler decreed frostily. 'And since Herr Busch is out of action, it'll be your turn tomorrow.'

Frau Mannheim tried to stage a tearful protest, but

Frau Köhler had already had the last word. She was a real dragon!

Opa made a swift recovery, but he could no longer cope with the weight of the water cans. Frau Mannheim took his place. I was pleased: from now on, Opa wouldn't have to expose himself to danger. Frau Mannheim was furious. She sought her husband's support, but he stayed out of the argument. The first time she set off with the cans, she made a great meal of it, walking with a limp and complaining.

'Cheer up, my love!' Herr Mannheim said.

When she reached the top of the stairs, Frau Mannheim announced that she hoped we would all be hit by an enormous bomb.

The incident with Opa's splinter coincided with the most dramatic period before the war ended.

A bomb hit the main supply of drinking water, and the whole of Berlin dried up. Once the barrels, buckets and cans were empty, the last resort was the river Spree. Out of necessity, people started to use that putrid water in which corpses floated. It was a miracle that none of us went down with typhus or dysentery.

We began to receive snippets of contradictory information that left us in a state of confusion. The BBC announced that the Soviets had broken through German lines in the East and were approaching the suburbs of Berlin; Deutscher Rundfunk, the official voice of the Reich, continued to reassure us that the Wenck Army 'was inflicting definitive defeat on the enemy'.

In fact, on 20 April, Hitler's birthday, Berlin came under direct Soviet artillery fire for the first time.

We had more reliable information from the people on the water rota. They told us that the city was in a state of uncontrolled chaos, and that there had been a massive invasion of rats. The streets were piled with corpses, and the stench was so terrible that people were fainting in the streets. None of the transport systems worked, not the tram or the omnibus or the *U-Bahn* or the elevated railway. The *U-Bahn* tunnel was crammed with people screaming with hunger and thirst, including tiny babies. There was no medical assistance of any kind, and medicine was impossible to find. We rummaged among the rubble to find anything to exchange on the black market, ignoring the sirens and defying death. Mass suicides were reported. Fear of the Russians had led many districts to build barricades and dig anti-personnel trenches. Anyone forced to leave the cellar for any reason was repeatedly stopped and searched.

Morale in the cellar had hit rock bottom. Peter was always sleepy, Kurt was forever shifting from a state of boredom to one of uncontrollable aggression. Erika had been left debilitated by her flu and still had a fever. Nonetheless, she was beautiful. Her skin was so transparent that the outlines of her bones showed through it. She had big forget-me-not blue eyes. She was so slim that she looked like the stem of a lily.

Erika's mother was a fine, courageous woman. One evening, after the blackout, she left the cellar armed with a little gun and a torch, and stayed out almost until dawn. In the meantime we had two air-raids, one of them very heavy. For hours we were worried that she wouldn't come back. But she finally returned with some good news. She had discovered a warehouse holding supplies for the *Wehrmacht*, where there were still large reserves of food. Our stepmother immediately suggested that we go there; Herr Spitzberg insisted on tagging along. Attempts were made to dissuade him, but for some strange reason he wouldn't let it drop. Opa didn't want Ursula to risk her life, but she had made up her mind.

The party decided to go out after dark. Those of us who stayed behind waited anxiously.

Opa, the poor man, was worried about his daughter; he paced up and down in the corridor. He reached the bucket and then turned around, hands clasped behind his back. I too was apprehensive, although I had to acknowledge that I was happier that my stepmother had gone rather than Opa.

They returned in the dead of night with a small barrel. Unfortunately Herr Spitzberg had been shot by a guard and died.

They had had to leave him behind. Erika's mother had killed the guard.

They lit a fire and cooked a vegetable soup with potatoes. For Erika there was some sweet condensed milk that would soon revive her.

We always had our ears cocked for noises coming from the top of the stairs, because we were afraid that the Gestapo or the SS might come looking for deserters. At the slightest hint, Kurt and one of the old men disappeared into a tunnel so well disguised that it would have been difficult for anyone, especially someone from outside the cellar, to find it. That was also where the radio was hidden.

Early one morning Opa heard on the radio that Soviet advance units had occupied the suburbs; I immediately thought of my boarding school in Eden. Opa said gravely, 'It won't be long now.' However, we were still tormented by bombing, day and night.

Our most recent supplies had improved Erika's condition, and she got a little colour back in her cheeks, giving fresh hope to her mother. Every now and again Herr Hammer would give Erika an encouraging look and say, 'Come on, little one, we'll soon have all this mess behind us!'

One day a young SS man stormed into our cellar. He had opened the door at the top of the stairs so quietly that we thought we were seeing a ghost. His face was white, and he was rolling his eyes. Crying 'All is lost, we are in the hands of the Bolsheviks. *Heil Hitler!*' he fired his gun into his mouth. Slumped at our feet, he had blood gushing from his face. Impassively, Herr Mannheim said, 'I'll sort it out.' Dragging the corpse away, he added it to the ones already keeping one another company by the shed.

We waited for the Russians; we knew they were bound to come, this was a rendezvous there was no getting out of. We couldn't think about anything else.

After a few days, Opa learned from the radio that the Soviets had occupied Tempelhof; at that point Ursula went up to Hilde's flat to call Aunt

Margarete's villa – the telephones worked right up until the end – but there was no reply. She tried again a number of times until she heard a Russian voice at the other end.

We waited in the little hell of our cellar. Terror was by now a habit, our constant companion; hunger and thirst a forced tribute to a cause that had proved some time ago to be nothing but a gigantic trap.

Meanwhile there was not a piece of lavatory paper to be found. Everything imaginable had been done to make up for that ridiculous shortage. We had cut up sheets and tea towels, and in the end we resorted to books, choosing the ones with the softest paper. Precious pages of Nietzsche and Shakespeare disappeared into the bucket. At first someone tried to keep our spirits up by joking about it, but he was soon silenced. 'When culture ends up in the shit,' said Herr Mannheim, 'a people is finished.'

Then came that terrible April night.

No sooner had I gone to sleep thinking about my father than I awoke with a sense that the cellar was shaking. I sat up and felt my heart hammering in my throat. Yes, the cellar was trembling to its foundations, and an indescribable din was assaulting our eardrums. Panic broke out, and shouts and curses against Hitler.

I was frozen with terror. The candle trembled nervously, casting terrible shadows as the battle raged above us. The Soviet heavy artillery was unleashed with such fury that it seemed to want to destroy the little that remained of the capital. Powerful explosions shook the walls like an earthquake. I began to shiver uncontrollably. I was sure that this was the end, that in a few minutes we would all be dead.

Herr Hammer stared at the ceiling as though willing it not to collapse, the veins in his neck swelling as they always did when he was frightened. All of a sudden a beam crashed on to Egon's bed; it looked as if the boy had been crushed! Luckily he had only fainted and was virtually unharmed. Frau Bittner wept convulsively with relief. Finally there was a terrible rumbling noise, and Herr Mannheim exclaimed, 'Damn it to Hell, this time it's our turn!' And he hugged his wife, weeping on her shoulder.

The cellar had filled with smoke, and we all started coughing. Erika's mother pressed a handkerchief to her daughter's mouth, but the poor thing was having a coughing fit.

We couldn't work out where the smoke was coming from, but we knew we were suffocating. My lungs felt as though they were full of sand. I coughed until I was sick. I glanced at my brother's bed, but it was empty. Then I saw Peter on our stepmother's camp bed, clinging to her like ivy. But I had Opa. He came over to my bed and asked me how I was. I did not know what to say. I was dreadfully upset. But so was he. He said, 'I don't know what's happening . . . my child . . . but you must try to . . . stay calm.' He was shouting because of the infernal noise. All of a sudden I saw him raise his hands to his head, roll his eyes and yell with a sob: 'I've had enough, I've got to get out of here, I've had enough!' He dashed off towards the stairs. My stepmother let go of Peter and ran after

Opa. Peter erupted into wails of protest and started to follow her. I leapt from my bed and grabbed my brother. Holding him tightly in my arms, I stammered, 'You're here, you're with me, you're here . . .'

He fought and kicked and stuck a fingernail in my eye, which immediately started bleeding copiously. When I tasted the blood my stomach lurched and I threw up on my brother.

Ursula had caught up with Opa and persuaded him to lie down on a camp bed. He started weeping like a child, and it broke my heart to see him. Finally he calmed down. The air-raid was over.

It had been the most violent attack we had suffered since the start of the war, and it had lasted for several hours. When the all-clear sounded, we all went out into the open to see what condition the building was in. It was still standing.

'The Soviets have reached the heart of Berlin,' Opa announced. We had just heard it on the BBC. 'We're finished,' he added. What would happen when the Russians found their way into our cellar? Although I didn't actually know what it meant, there was much talk of rape. Frau Bittner was worried about her daughter, even though she was a mere shadow of a girl. In fact, neither my stepmother, Frau Köhler nor Frau Bittner herself were old women.

Having heard the news, Rudolf, Frau Köhler's son, underwent a complete change of character. Suddenly filled with concern for his mother, he wanted to know precisely what rape was, after which he forbade her to leave the cellar.

The centre of Berlin was packed with armoured cars; bullets were flying everywhere. The Russians were heading for the Reichstag.

Opa and Herr Mannheim were constantly glued to the radio, trying to pick their way through the flood of information. Deutscher Rundfunk was suddenly interrupted one day, right in the middle of a news item. The silence that followed could mean only one thing: the enemy had captured the radio station.

For days no-one had left the cellar. Our supplies were exhausted.

We spent most of our time lying on our beds to save our strength. On the one hand we hoped that the war would end, while on the other we dreaded the arrival of the Russians. Meanwhile the bombs kept falling. None of us could guess what important buildings might still be standing that would act as a lure to the enemy. Berlin was a bonfire now, what more did they want?

Hilde had not been seen for a week. My stepmother had phoned the Ministry, but they didn't know where she was. Opa and my stepmother were very concerned.

XIV

Throughout those months of 1945, I concentrated my strength on surviving. It was not that my mind had dried up or that my need for love had been satisfied; quite the contrary. I simply had other priorities. You can get by without love but not without food and water. I had locked away my desire for love, waiting for better times, times I would in fact never know. Even after the war my stepmother would reject me, excluding me from my family; my father would submit to her wishes.

I never gave my real mother a second thought now. Sometimes I found myself thinking nostalgically of my grandmother and my father, but I had erased my mother from my memory. I would only confront the black hole she had left in my thoughts many years later, when I had a child of my own.

We waited for the Russians with mounting apprehension. As the days passed, that waiting became a barely containable anxiety; we hardly thought about anything else. The adults did their best to put on a brave face, but fear lay over the cellar like a suffocating blanket, keeping us from sleep. I often thought of the Russians Hans and I had met in Eden and who had given us semolina and bread: they hadn't seemed such bad people. I convinced myself that there must be two kinds of Russians: the ones we had met in Eden and the 'Soviets' that Goebbels called primitive barbarians. Perhaps when the 'Russians' arrived, I thought, there wouldn't be too much to fear.

One day as he was waiting for her – she had gone to fetch some water – Rudolf, Frau Köhler's twelve-year-old son, had started talking about rape; he had become unbearable. He tormented everyone with his insane fears for his mother.

Suddenly he leapt to his feet, walked over to Opa and ask him for a gun. Opa asked what he wanted it for. To kill the first Russian who dared to lay his paws on his mother, Rudolf replied, his face pale and grim. Opa explained that he was unable to comply with his wishes, first of all because he was only a boy and secondly because weapons were not permitted in shelters. Rudolf lost his temper and started shouting, saying the men in the cellar were cowards because they had no intention of defending the women from the Russians. Opa repeated that the Russians would come armed to the teeth and, if they did find weapons, would slaughter the lot of us.

Rudolf was far from convinced and responded insolently. The others tried to calm him down but to no avail. His fury only subsided when Frau Köhler returned with the water cans. I no longer recognised him. The mild-mannered boy who spent hours ruining his eyesight reading Karl May by candle-light had turned into a raging insurrectionary.

Frau Köhler asked her son, 'Has something happened, darling?'

Rudolf glanced at Opa, who said calmly, 'No, Frau Köhler. Your son was just a bit worried because you were late.'

Frau Köhler sighed and said, 'It's hell out there. There is gunfire all over the place; you have to be very careful not to get shot. Armoured cars everywhere, and Hitler Youth trying to stop them with Panzer-fausts . . . Those poor boys are dying like flies, it's a scandal!' She stroked her son's hair, gave him an affectionate biff on the nose, lay down on the camp bed and went to sleep.

I watched Frau Köhler as she slept. Her face looked drained, her cheeks were sunken, her eyes were two black holes. She resembled a death-mask.

I shuddered. Frau Köhler was not an old woman, but at times she looked ancient! The same could be said of the other women, my stepmother included. It was as though some malicious hand had wiped their faces of any residual memory of lost youth. My step-mother, who was not yet thirty, had changed to a terrifying degree. I remembered the first time I had seen her standing next to my father: her very blue eyes, slightly hard but intelligent and lively; the sober, easy elegance of a young woman who had grown up in a metropolis. Her body, slender yet soft, her bold, slightly arrogant smile; my father had liked her, oh, how he had liked her! He had liked everything about her, and he had made no secret of the fact.

Opa was talking to Ursula. They were worried

about Hilde; no-one knew what had happened to her. Perhaps she had been hit by a shell on her way home. Or perhaps, surprised by an air-raid, she had slipped into a shelter that had subsequently been blown up. My stepmother kept saying we should send out a search party, although they both realised that the authorities would not be keen to set off on a wild goose chase unless the person in question was a Jew sought by the Gestapo.

I stretched out on the bed and listened as they talked in the hot, fetid cellar. In the end sleep got the better of me, and I nodded off while Herr Mannheim calculated that the Russians wouldn't come for two or three days, because they were still too busy laying siege to the Reichstag.

I awoke to suspicious noises at the top of the stairs and raised the alarm. Kurt and the old man immediately slipped into the tunnel; everyone who had been dozing woke up with a start. Two seconds later we found ourselves face to face with six Russian soldiers, all aiming submachine-guns at us.

I felt like I was watching a film. Everything had happened so quickly that it took me a couple of seconds to grasp what was going on. The Russians stared at us and then looked around them. They were clearly disgusted by the stench but at the same time amazed at the sight of our encampment. We were all frozen to the spot.

I saw round, pink faces. Two of them had shaven heads, three wore fur caps, and one had black, curly hair and a beard that came down over his chest. The man with the beard asked peremptorily: 'Here *soldaty germanskie?*' Petrified, no-one answered.

'*Soldaty germanskie?*' the bearded man repeated impatiently.

Opa, forcing himself to stay calm, said, 'No soldiers here.'

'You lie!'

'No lie, here no soldiers.'

The bearded man, deliberately articulating his words, said, 'If *soldaty germanskie* here, you *kaputt!*' Staring Opa in the eye, he added, 'Understand?'

'I understand,' Opa replied, and tried to dispel the tension. 'Here only old people, women and children.'

The Russian stared at him for a few seconds, then glanced quickly around the desolate cellar. Finally he asked, 'You weapons?' He had very black, intelligent eyes and a red, fleshy mouth. All six of the men looked well-fed and healthy.

'No weapons,' Opa replied. A shiver ran down my spine. The Russian took another look around; there was something strange in his eyes, a kind of baffled disbelief. He contemplated the wretched beds, the wooden table with the suitcases underneath, holding our few valuables and a few clothes, the smoking candle, Erika clutching her tureen, the beds where Egon and Peter still slept. Suddenly a grin of triumph spread across his face, and he exclaimed, 'War *kaputt!* Hitler *kaputt!*' He assessed our reactions. Seeing only fear, he asked in a businesslike voice: 'You *urri?*'

Peter and Egon had woken up and were both weeping with fear. The bearded man nodded for someone to tend to the little boys and repeated, more harshly: 'You *urri*!' He tapped his wrist with two fingers. Finally we understood, and everyone with a watch hurried to slip it off his wrist. Only the old man who was always wetting himself put up any resistance: 'Not my watch! It's all I have to remind me of my wife . . . I can't give you my watch!' He wept, writhing in desperation. One of the Russians aimed his gun between the old man's eyes. 'You give *urri* or you *kaputt*!' But the old man went on whining with an obstinacy that had become ridiculous.

'Give up the watch, you fool,' whispered Herr Hammer.

The old man choked and snivelled.

Then the Russian said contemptuously, 'You cry for *urri*? You *idiot*! Better you weep for your city!' He brutally slipped the watch from the old man's wrist.

My stepmother and Frau Bitttner had hurried to the beds of the two tearful little boys, trying to reassure them. The bearded man, staring first at Opa and then at me, ordered, '*Idi syuda!*' We didn't understand. He beckoned us over. The man smiled broadly and said to Opa, 'You *gut*!' Turning to me, he asked, 'You *golod*?' He made an eating gesture. I was unable to speak.

'You *golod*?' he repeated, raising his voice.

'Tell him you're hungry,' Opa suggested.

'Yes,' I said breathily.

The Russian said something to one of the other men, who slipped a loaf of black bread out of a knapsack and handed it to me. When he saw my embarrassed amazement, he laughed. He stroked my cheek with the butt of his rifle and said something to the others. They all laughed. They laughed in the dark and stinking cellar, and I couldn't tell whether they were laughing with amusement or pity. Then the bearded man said, 'You say *spasibo*.' I didn't understand.

Opa came to my aid. 'It means "thank you", darling. Thank him.'

'Thank you.'

'*Spasibo!*' he said again, and the other Russians echoed him: '*Spasibo! Spasibo! Da!*'

In a thin voice I said, '*Spasibo*.'

Finally satisfied, they left us, yelling 'Hitler *kaputt*! Germany *kaputt*!' The words echoed darkly around the filthy cellar.

There was a stunned silence. Then relief. Bewildered agitation. Restorative sneezing. Herr Hammer blew his nose with a page of Nietzsche and murmured, 'That was lucky!' Finally everyone was talking at once, and there was a mood of jubilation. I pressed the loaf to my chest as though it were a baby. 'I want the bread!' Peter shrilled, hugging both me and it.

Frau Köhler, once she had recovered from the shock, exclaimed, 'If those are the barbarians Goebbels was talking about, they've got my vote!'

Hopping about, Egon said, 'I want some bread too!'

The two men hiding in the tunnel were called out. 'Out you come, deserters and *soldaty germanskie*!' someone joked.

Opa took the bread from me and started to cut it into as many slices as there were people in the cellar. We consumed our slices slowly, relishing every last crumb. I thought I had never eaten anything more exquisite.

When everyone had relaxed a bit, the adults discussed the possibility that Hitler might be dead.

'That would be too good to be true,' said Frau Köhler.

'And they didn't touch any of the women!' sobbed Frau Mannheim. The two mothers hugged one another because their daughters were out of danger. Opa and Herr Mannheim withdrew into the tunnel to hear the latest news on the radio. The noose around Berlin was tightening, the city was about to fall. We all felt we had been saved by a miracle. The sirens hadn't sounded for ages: that seemed like a good sign.

Exhausted by fear, most of us took to our beds. Peter curled up near our stepmother on her camp bed. Opa paid me a compliment. 'You have been very brave, my child.'

Grateful and proud, I replied, 'Thank you.' Then I corrected myself: '*Spasibo*.'

Opa smiled, touched and amused. 'I'm proud of you.' Ursula hadn't said a word to me, but Opa's pride made me very happy.

XV

Berlin, end of April 1945

I awoke to the sound of excited chatter. Frau Köhler
was talking to a woman I didn't know. Their faces
were anxious. Suddenly Rudolf started yelling, 'I want
a gun! You've got to give me a gun!'

I felt confused. After the Russians' visit, I must have
slept like a baby, but now there clearly was another
problem.

The woman was a childhood friend of Frau Köhler
who was hiding in a cellar not far away, near
Lauenburger Platz. She had come to warn us that
groups of drunken Russians were wandering the
district molesting women.

The news came like a thunderbolt out of a peaceful
sky, and panic began to spread. In exasperated fury,
Opa grabbed a glass and hurled it to the floor,
shouting, 'Damn it to Hell! How could we have been
so naïve?' Hugging my stepmother, he wept on her
shoulder. Poor man! He was already apprehensive
about Hilde and now, on top of everything, there was
the threat of rape!

We put our heads together: what was to be done?

Should we pretend the women were ill? Hide them on the top floors of the building? Someone recommended hiding them among the corpses in the courtyard, but Frau Köhler said she would rather be killed. Rudolf kept repeating that he wanted a pistol to protect his mother.

The commotion woke Peter, who, seeing that no-one was paying him any attention, started rocking back and forth on the bed-springs, making an irritating squeaking sound.

'Stop it, Peter!' Ursula cried.

'No!'

She went over to the bed and slapped him on the bottom. Peter stared at her in disbelief and burst into furious tears. Egon joined in and the tense situation became even more volatile. Fortunately their tears only lasted long enough to exhaust their surplus energy.

'There's always the tunnel,' Frau Köhler remarked suddenly. 'It's safe in there.'

'I don't know how you'd get six people into that tunnel,' Herr Hammer objected. 'There's room for three at the most.'

Helpless bewilderment spread through the cramped cellar. Tired faces, fear, dismay. What was to be done? Two seconds later, like staggering ghosts, two Russians appeared, obviously drunk. They came unsteadily towards us, singing and trying to dance. One of them was wearing a fur cap that sat crookedly on his head, the other had a thicket of red hair and a stubbly beard. I flattened myself on the bed to avoid being noticed.

The Russians chortled and swung their rifles around. They gestured to me to get down off the bed. Then they did the same to Egon and Peter. Egon burst into tears, while Peter climbed down submissively. The Russians stared perplexedly at us, as though we were circus animals. Finally one of them emitted a series of belches and bellowed, 'You *urri*?' Not again, I thought. No-one moved.

'You *urri*!' repeated the Russian, growing impatient. Showing his bare wrist and inviting the others to do the same, Opa tried to explain that we had already been relieved of our watches. The Russian then began to shine his torch our faces, paying particular attention to the women. When he came to my stepmother, he stopped and shouted, 'Hurrah Stalin!', dazzling her with the torch. With Peter clinging to her legs, my stepmother didn't move.

The Russian belched again and defiantly repeated, 'Hurrah Stalin!', laying a heavy hand on her shoulder. Once again she showed no reaction. The other Russian, vexed by her silence, ordered, 'You say "Hurrah Stalin", or you *kaputt*!' Peter choked down a frightened sob, but Opa saved the situation by standing in for his daughter: 'Hurrah Stalin!'

The Russian turned, his face widening into a smile of satisfaction. 'You *gut*!' Belching complacently, he asked, 'Your wife?', pointing to Ursula.

'I am the father,' Opa replied. '*Ich bin der Vater.*'

'*Vater*?' The Russian frowned, struggled to think, stared at a button on his dusty uniform and finally observed: '*Vater gut!* You say again "Hurrah Stalin!" You *Vater gut*! *Da*!'

'Hurrah Stalin!' said Opa.

The Russian looked at him with delight, slapped his thigh and bellowed: 'Again! Again "Hurrah Stalin!"' He fixed Opa with bright, reddened eyes.

When Opa obeyed for the third time, my heart clenched. Poor Opa!

Finally the Russian was satisfied, and his face became comically serious. With a confidential gesture, he rested a great paw on Opa's bony shoulder and said, 'Hitler *kaputt*!' He mimed someone shooting himself in the temple and added, grinding his teeth, 'Hitler grrrr! Adolf *kaputt*!' And he whinnied like a horse, laughing with his head thrown back.

The other Russian chanted cheerfully, '*Alles kaputt! Germaniya kaputt! Parlament kaputt! Da!*' and slapped his comrade repeatedly on the shoulder. But his comrade was distracted; he was staring at Erika.

All of a sudden the Russian with the cap aimed his rifle at my chest and thundered: '*Imya! Name! Was . . . dein . . . Name?*'

I felt my throat dry up as a toad lumbered about in my poor guts.

'Tell him your name, darling,' Opa whispered.

'Helga,' I murmured.

'Gelga?'

'Helga.'

The Russian scratched his head: 'You are *gut*, Gelga.' He came towards me, his breath stinking, and touched my flat chest. I wondered why he was touching me. I was tempted to bite his hand, but I managed to control myself. Finally the beast squeezed one of my nipples and said contemptuously, 'No, Gelga no *gut*!' He spat on the floor and let me go. Moving on to Gudrun, he said gleefully, 'You *Fräulein*! You *gut*! You come with me!' Gudrun's mother hurled herself at him. 'No, you can't do that. Please, take me instead, I beg you, she's just a child!' But the Russian kicked her violently in the stomach: 'Bitch!'

Frau Bittner fell backwards, striking her head. She lay on the ground, apparently unconscious. The others flocked around to help her. I was afraid I was going to vomit. The Russian, taking advantage of the hubbub, dragged Gudrun into the corridor, gesturing to his comrade to keep us at a distance with his submachine-gun. The other man ordered us to stand in a line and leave Frau Bittner on the ground, 'otherwise *kaputt*'. We had no choice but to obey him.

Gudrun's agonising cries rang out in the corridor, seeming to explode in our heavy hearts. I wanted to die.

The Russian returned from the corridor. He looked at us with an expression of arrogant satisfaction, but when he saw our unanimous contempt, his face altered. He finished buttoning his trousers, grunting with embarrassment, finally giving us a smile of overbearing gratification, muttering something in his language. Switching places with him, the other Russian went and sat, swaying, next to Erika. It had never until that moment occurred to me that a man might take the slightest interest in such a shadow of a girl.

Erika stared at the Russian and turned white as a

sheet. She started trembling, and her coughs mingled with her tears.

'Your name!' shouted the Russian, rocking from side to side and slobbering.

Erika moved her lips but couldn't utter a word. The Russian repeated impatiently: 'Your name!'

The poor girl swallowed, took a deep breath and stammered 'E-ri-ka.'

'Erika . . .' said the Russian, lifting a lock of her hair with the butt of his rifle. She gave a start, and, as a sob shook her, the tureen slipped from her hands and shattered with an infernal crash.

A confused expression crossed the Russian's face as he stared at the fragments. Then he gripped Erika by the shoulders and tried to kiss her. Her mother threw herself at him, pleading, 'I beg you, take me in her place . . . she is ill . . . she . . .' The man struck her violently on the head with his gun. She slumped heavily to the floor, unconscious.

The Russian flung Erika on to a mattress, throwing his whole weight on top of her. Someone went to help Erika's mother, but the Russian with the gun shouted something and fired into the air. The report rang out in the dark. I tried to take my eyes off the horrible spectacle, but I couldn't. What I saw was unimaginable, cruel, unjust. When I was able to cry, I buried my face in Opa's jacket.

XVI

The Russians left, slapping each other on the back and bellowing with sated laughter. A moment of confused silence followed. The two mothers in a dead faint, Erika groaning on the mattress; I fled into the corridor. Gudrun was there, and I was swept aside by everyone running to help her. She lay curled up on her side, eyes staring, face frozen in pain.

They carried her to one of the camp beds, covering her with sheets and coats. She was trembling, her teeth were chattering, and her eyes were wide and staring. The two mothers were semi-conscious.

Someone went upstairs to find out whether there was any kind of first-aid service for rape victims, but there wasn't. No such thing existed. Nothing existed now. Nothing but horror. The mood in the cellar was one of impotent fury and impotent compassion.

On Erika's mattress was a patch of blood the size of an apple. I stared at it in astonishment; it was as though what had happened somehow involved me, too. I decided that no man would ever touch me; men were nothing but ferocious beasts, apart from the ones in our cellar.

Meanwhile Erika was crouching on the floor, trembling, coughing and covering herself with her hands. A blanket had been put around her shoulders, but she kept throwing it off.

The moment the Russians left, Peter and Egon had fallen into a deep sleep. I don't know how much they took in of what had happened, but, at least as far as Peter was concerned, I never heard him ask any questions about it. Kurt, Gudrun's brother, was racked with guilt for not defending his sister. In fact there was no way he could have helped her; the Russians would have killed him.

I was still staring at the bloodstain when my stepmother said to me, 'Don't look at it!' I asked her why.

'Just don't!' came her usual imperious reply. But this time I didn't accept it. 'Tell me why!' I insisted.

'Because you might not forget it, that's why!'

'I don't want to forget!' I answered, although I wasn't really clear about why. Twitching with rage, she gripped a lock of her dirty hair in her fist. 'It's better to forget!'

I was about to disagree, but Peter had woken up and was demanding attention, so she went to him.

Meanwhile the two mothers had recovered sufficiently to attend to their respective daughters. Erika's mother persuaded her to lie on a camp bed, and one of the old men laid a worn military blanket over the stained mattress. But all the maternal love in the world would not have been enough to bring relief to Erika. It was as though her body, shattered by the horrible abuse to which she had been subjected, had succumbed to her illness. Struggling against a terrible

164

breathlessness, lips bloodless and eyes vacant, she coughed and spat blood into a tin bowl someone had brought to her.

Later there was a heavy artillery attack. I spent the night in a state of anxiety somewhere between waking and sleeping. An agitated murmur made me sit up. The women were gathering around Erika's camp bed. She was losing blood.

I heard the word *haemorrhage* echo threateningly. Frau Köhler tore up a sheet and put a strip of it between Erika's legs, but the frequency with which the women replaced the pieces of torn sheet suggested that something serious was happening. All of a sudden Erika's mother burst into desperate tears and ran upstairs in search of help.

There was another air-raid warning, and we were hit by furious shelling. An unusual roaring resounded heavily in the cellar, as though someone had just unloaded several tons of coal. Having gone upstairs, Herr Hammer came back with the news that someone had blocked the door from outside. I saw fresh dismay on everyone's faces. We could not stay there with the door blocked, and besides, we were waiting for Erika's mother to come back!

At first light, Opa, Herr Hammer, the Mannheims and Frau Köhler decided to go and unblock the door. My stepmother stayed with Frau Bittner, who was shuttling back and forth between Erika and Gudrun; I followed the others very quietly.

Day was breaking, the air was still and veiled with shimmering red as the city burned. For a moment I lingered in the courtyard, tired and numb with cold.

But all of a sudden a blinding shaft of light burst over the ruins. The sun was coming up, and a wayward beam lit the railings of a balcony that clung tenaciously to the façade of a bombed-out building. A solitary bird began to call. A section of a staircase could be seen, with rats running about on it, a piece of kitchen with the sink still fixed to the wall, and an item of clothing, perhaps an apron, absurdly attached to a hook on the unhinged door. Herr Mannheim clambered over the rubble, hoping to find some tools in the shed, while the others started to clear the debris blocking our door.

An old man passing on a ramshackle bicycle stopped to ask us what we were doing. Exhausted, he said he had escaped from a special squad that had been wiped out in less than three hours, and that he no longer cared whether he was seen to be a deserter. Dressed in rags and skeletally thin, he seemed utterly worn out. There was a suppurating wound on his neck. He told us the *U-Bahn* was packed with people moaning with hunger and thirst; they were dying like flies, and the dead were being thrown on to the rails as they began to decompose. He had heard that troops were closing in on Berlin, that many thousands of cannon were aimed at the capital and that corpses were being buried in every courtyard. As he jumped on his bone-shaker and left without saying goodbye, Herr Hammer exploded: 'I said we should have buried the corpses in our courtyard; we would have been spared the stench!'

This made the concierge very angry: 'Who is responsible for this building? I am! So no-one is going to bury as much as a mouse in our courtyard, you understand? I keep to the rules, I do!'

'But who on earth keeps to the rules anymore?' bleated Frau Mannheim, rubbing her knee.

'We do!' roared Frau Köhler, adding slyly, 'You know what's going to happen the minute the war's over? All the sly ones who disobeyed the rules will be forced to dig up those poor corpses for identification! The Allies will want to know how many Germans have kicked the bucket!'

We finished freeing the front door and went down into the cellar to ask after the two girls. Gudrun had not moved. Erika was wheezing. We feared for her life and for that of her mother as well, since she still hadn't come back.

When daylight came, Frau Mannheim went out to fetch the water, complaining endlessly. But she came back straight away, saying that she had met two women who were looking for an address where there was said to be a warehouse that was still reasonably well stocked with food. Ursula and Frau Köhler immediately decided to go there. Half an hour later we were subjected to furious shelling, but as though by a miracle our building remained standing.

Finally Ursula, Frau Köhler and Erika's mother came back. My stepmother had lost a shoe. Their booty was meagre, because the warehouse had already been attacked by the *Volkssturm* militia, who had made off with most of the food. There had been a terrible crush. Frau Köhler had a black eye.

Frau Bittner cooked everyone a pot of steaming semolina over a fire made from some furniture she had collected in the cellar, and while Opa was massaging his daughter's sore foot, an old man appeared, dragging a rusty racing bicycle. He informed us that Hilde was in a military hospital to which she had been taken after being caught by an air-raid in the street: she had been hit in the side by shrapnel. Opa and my stepmother were greatly relieved. Where was the hospital? The old man wouldn't tell us, because it was in a part of the city where there was still a great deal of fighting, and Hilde didn't want them to risk their lives trying to find her. 'When things have calmed down,' the old man assured us, 'you will find out where she is.' Politely refusing any semolina, he dragged his bicycle back up the stairs and went on his way.

Erika's mother returned with an old lady doctor leaning on a stick; she could hardly move. She wore thick glasses, and her face was framed by a grey braid held in place with a large number of horn hairpins. All of a sudden Erika opened her eyes and smiled. Her mother asked, 'Are you better, my love?'

Erika nodded, her face pale as alabaster.

'I've brought a doctor, darling,' her mother said.

The doctor examined the girl as we all gathered around the camp bed.

Eventually Erika looked up at us one by one, smiled weakly and murmured, 'Thank you.' Then her lips tensed, her eyelids grew heavy, a long shudder ran through her body, and a drop of blood appeared at the corner of her mouth, like a tiny rosebud. She gripped her mother's hand and kissed it. But the kiss stiffened, and she died biting her mother's fingers.

XVII

Berlin, beginning of May 1945

Erika's death left us despondent.

With the help of the old doctor, her mother managed a decent burial for the poor girl, who knows how. The corpse was taken away in a little white bathroom cabinet with the drawers and legs removed. After this, life in the cellar seemed to stop. Not even my memories could console me.

I had lost any sense of the past: my grandmother, Aunt Margarete, cousin Eva, my father, Eden, everything had turned into a shapeless lump. I had Opa, but he was not always in the mood to chat.

It was at around this time that we learned from our radio that Hitler had died in the bunker of the Reich Chancellery.

The Russians turned up in our cellar three more times. Of course they were a threat, but theoretically the SS could also appear at any moment to recruit some poor wretch for their squads.

Four Russian officers arrived towards evening, covered with medals. Clean-shaven, brisk and correct.

Soldaty germanskie? Urri? Guns? *Do svidaniya!* They didn't touch the women.

The following morning it was the turn of seven soldiers. Two of them were Mongolian in appearance, with cunning, slanted eyes and stocky bodies. One was blond and extremely handsome, Hitler would have been delighted. *Urri?* Guns? *Soldaty germanskie?* No rapes. No bread.

Last to come were a trio. One wore a mouth-organ around his neck. They searched the cellar from top to bottom without finding the tunnel. They also spared the women. Great relief all round, and a boost to our morale.

An old man from a cellar two blocks away would come and see us just for a chat. He seemed slightly mad and very lonely, but he told us lots of things. For example, that many women from our district had been raped by the Russians, and that some men had been killed for trying to defend them. He said that the SS were committing suicide in large numbers because they couldn't bear the idea of falling into the hands of the Soviets.

The old man came often: perhaps he found our cellar more companionable than the one where he had taken shelter after fleeing, without his family, from eastern Germany. He told us that as the Red Army marched towards Berlin, it had literally carpeted the villages it passed through with portraits of Stalin, planting red banners everywhere and defying the people to remove them. One day this sprightly story-teller with a dark sense of humour made me laugh. He said, 'The stench of corpses in Berlin might even be bearable if it weren't for the stench of the living!'

It had become practically impossible to leave the cellar without getting ourselves killed. Berlin had become a gigantic battlefield: rockets, shells and artillery fire of all kinds and calibres rained down from all directions. No-one ventured out any more, not even to fetch water. To make matters worse, our food supplies were running out. All that remained were some dried peas that we boiled up over a wood fire, producing intolerable quantities of smoke that made us cough furiously and left our eyes streaming. In the end we ate them almost raw.

We were all weak and reaching the end of our endurance. The bucket was increasingly deserted. We were seized by an overwhelming desire to sleep which kept us fixed in our beds. Peter and Egon looked like little twigs with their sap dried up. I had not had much, just Eden, but at least I knew the blue of the sky and the sweetness of ripe apples, the euphoria of going as high as I could on a swing, and the tangy smell of newly mown grass. All Peter knew were barred windows, a terrible stench, desperate crowding and a bed made of two tables jammed together!

Frau Köhler's friend, the one who had warned us of the arrival of the drunken Russians, ran down into the cellar and left us a can of water. She saved our lives.

'Where did you get it, Lotte?' Frau Köhler asked her.

Her friend smiled cunningly. 'We brought back about ten of them!'

'Where on earth did you find it?'

'In a giant barrel buried in the bloody garden of a bloody Nazi!' Lotte exploded. Frau Köhler hugged her friend. 'Oh, Lotte, Lotte, you haven't changed one bit! Have you any idea what this means to us? Is there any water left in the barrel?'

'I wouldn't advise you to leave the cellar,' her friend replied. 'We got away with it by a miracle. If you had any idea of the chaos out there! We've seen things you wouldn't believe! The centre of the city looks like an anthill; there are military vehicles, ambulances, camouflaged trucks, armoured cars, all charging blindly about the place, crushing everything in their path, driving over corpses . . . I tell you, it's an inferno! The air is full of ash, the soot sticks to your hair, and there's gunfire coming from all directions! It's crazy! And there are injured people everywhere asking for help! I saw a boy from the Hitler Youth, he must have been about thirteen, leaning against a tree with his guts spilling out. It's better if I don't tell you . . .' And off she ran, hat crooked and shoes full of holes.

I lay on my bed and stared at the water-pipe. Then I started looking at the cobweb instead, at the spider busying himself weaving. He was spreading his web, weaving and waiting for the female spider to appear.

She usually emerged full tilt from behind the water-pipe to inspect the web in all its glory before stopping all of a sudden and falling into a profound meditation. Maybe she wanted to destroy the web to make one of her own, perhaps according to some extravagant design? Or perhaps the couple were trying to decide how best to create a nursery for their young.

After a while I heard Egon asking his mother for some water. Lotte's supply had run out the day before, and no-one had gone out to bring back any more.

Frau Bittner asked Egon to hold out a little longer. Once the situation outside was safer, someone would go and fetch water. But he wouldn't listen. He fell out of bed, bringing on a series of convulsions that lasted for half an hour. When he had recovered, his mother took the cans and went upstairs. Kurt objected, but she was gone without a backward look.

In less than three minutes she was back. Putting down the cans, she slipped into a chair, ashen pale. Herr Hammer sat up on his camp bed, sneezed several times and asked in his cold-ridden voice, 'What's happening, Frau Bittner, do you feel ill?'

She shook her head, caught a hairpin that was falling out of her hair, thoughtfully fixed it up again and replied, 'The war is over.'

It was as though a fuse had been lit. 'What?' cried Herr Hammer, leaping from his bed. 'Who told you?'

'They're shouting it outside.'

Opa ran to the radio. He came back almost immediately, his face radiant: 'Berlin has surrendered. The war is over!'

There was an explosion of jubilation, tears of disbelief flowed down our faces. Euphoria, kisses, tears. Frau Mannheim, whom I had never seen smiling, was so overjoyed that she displayed her gap of three missing teeth. Herr Hammer sneezed and wept. Peter burst into tears because he couldn't understand why there was so much noise. Egon cried and begged for some water. Gudrun had got up but couldn't speak. I had a great lump in my throat, and went and hugged Opa.

All of a sudden everything was erased: quarrels, insults, meanness and intolerance, malice and vulgar jokes, sullenness, a lack of solidarity, of sensitivity, of humanity. The cellar could not contain our happiness, and we rushed into the street.

People ran towards us, and there was more hugging and laughing and crying I felt wonderful, an overwhelming, uncontainable joy. My stepmother hugged me and murmured, overcome with emotion, 'Everything will be all right, you'll see.' More and more people were shouting, 'The war is over! The war is over!' They were ghosts drunk with joy. Surrender had turned us into human beings again, sanctioning the first of our rights, the right to hope. We weren't just survivors, we were new people.

But what was Berlin like now? It was an expanse of burning ruins whose glow turned night to day. A limitless bonfire with a residue of humanity enduring the most catastrophic conditions in its belly. The streets were packed with corpses that stank to the heavens; the water shortage had turned the city into an open-air latrine. For a long time there had been no electricity, or gas, or water, or heating, or any distribution of food or medicine; the sewers were paralysed. Infectious diseases raged, so lice, bugs and rats reigned supreme. No-one had been going to school, no-one was working. Poor spectral figures, filthy and covered in rags, weakened in mind and body, emerged from cellars, shelters and the *U-Bahn*. They were Germans, representatives of the master race. In reality they were nothing but shadows.

The cellar was hastily cleared, and the mattresses were carried back up into the block. The suitcases returned to the flats, this time forever.

Opa called me from the top of the stairs, suitcase in hand. We were the last ones to leave.

I gazed around the empty space where we had lived crammed on top of one another, piled up like beasts, intruding on our neighbours with our smells, our bad tempers, our selfishness. We had passed beyond what was endurable, what was imaginable; we had passed beyond our strength, beyond humanity. Yet we were to learn that our suffering was nothing compared with what had happened to the Jews in the concentration camps.

'Helga!' Opa called. 'Let's go.'

I took the candle and joined him.

Outside the door to Hilde's flat, he asked, 'What were you doing down there? Had you forgotten something?'

'I was just looking,' I replied. 'I was looking so I wouldn't forget anything.'

He stroked my hair, murmuring, 'You're a special girl,' and slid the key into the lock.

XVIII

Berlin, May 1945

Because Erika's mother had nowhere to go, Opa offered her hospitality in Hilde's flat until she could find accommodation elsewhere. The poor thing, inconsolable about the death of her daughter, planned to ask the occupying authorities for permission to return to her village, but that would take some time to sort out because the city was in total chaos.

Once the war was over, Peter and I were convinced that everything would be fine, that there would be electricity, food and water. It was not to be. There was still a water shortage, and Ursula was forced to trade her most precious jewels on the black market in Alexanderplatz for a small supply of provisions.

Hour no longer followed unchanging hour; the rhythm of our lives returned to normal. We slept at night rather than during the day, although for the first little while the unfamiliar nocturnal silence kept me awake. Sometimes I worried that the war was not really over, that we might be surprised by a sudden air-raid in the middle of the night. I still worried about being killed.

The flat was arranged very satisfactorily. Erika's mother slept in the small bedroom, our stepmother on a little folding bed in Hilde's study, along with the piano and my father's painting, Opa was on the sofa in the sitting-room, and Peter and I slept on camp beds in the dining room. We planned to stay in Lothar Bucher Strasse until Hilde returned from the military hospital, and perhaps even during her convalescence, which I hoped would take a long time; I didn't want to go back to Friedrichsruher Strasse with Ursula! Nothing between us had changed, I could feel it.

The Soviet administration set up its headquarters in Berlin, and General Berzarin was put in charge of the garrison and the city. He posted ordinances on the walls and advertising pillars, and also had fliers distributed asking the population to adhere scrupulously to the regulations of the Soviet occupying force, giving an assurance that ration cards would soon be distributed. People were also told not to leave their districts, and not to leave their homes between 10:00 at night and 8:00 in the morning. Initially, clocks (any that had escaped the Russians' indiscriminate plundering) had to be set to Moscow time, but subsequently we were allowed to return to local time. For a short while, once the euphoria had worn off, the adults around me seemed lost, as though they were in some sort of shock. Survival still seemed to be their sole preoccupation. Everything was in a state of suspension. No newspapers were published; the radio broadcast nothing but music. There was no other source of information. The former capital of the Third Reich was an island cut off from the rest of the world.

Soon the water supply was restored and the electrical plants rebuilt. Hilde came home, and it was a very happy and emotional moment for Opa and my stepmother. But Hilde was pale and emaciated, still unwell. She walked with her shoulders bent, dragging one leg; her mouth twisted when she laughed. She looked like a little old woman. She spent the first few days in bed in a room whose wall had collapsed. It looked as though her convalescence was going to take a fairly long time.

What had become of our community in the cellar in Lothar Bucher Strasse? Nothing. Everyone lived for himself, and not even the tenants of the same building nurtured any particular feelings of friendship for one another. It seemed, in fact, as though their long period of forced confinement had led them in the opposite direction.

The authorities granted Erika's mother permission to return to her village, and we were all very touched to see her setting off with the cardboard suitcase in which she still kept her poor daughter's clothes. Herr Hammer locked himself away in his little flat, and only ever showed his face when he needed to ask the concierge something. Frau Köhler took charge of her porter's lodge again, working day and night to make the communal spaces inhabitable. Rudolf discovered football and ran wild in the courtyard once the corpses, or what remained of them, had been removed. The Mannheims became exiles within their own four walls, only ever exchanging a few hasty words with Frau Bittner about Gudrun. The poor thing still had not recovered the power of speech, and her mother had arranged an appointment for her in a sanatorium that had recently opened in Steglitz.

It soon became apparent that rationing would only just keep us from dying of hunger. To win the right to increased rations, our stepmother volunteered to clear the streets of rubble. And because I had been diagnosed with malnutrition, I was entitled to supplementary stamps. Of course Peter claimed that he had a similar ailment, and for a few days beat himself up with a paperweight, leaving himself with horrible bruises.

Now that we had running water again, we were always well scrubbed. Not elegant, perhaps, but clean at least. Peter's silky curls had started to flourish again, and Ursula's hair regained its former ash-blonde colour. From time to time she wore her turban, not to cover her dirty hair but to protect her clean hair from the dust when clearing away rubble. Opa was happy to be able to wear ironed clothes again. Hilde no longer talked about her time at the Propaganda Ministry. Any mention of Goebbels, Hitler or Nazism was forbidden.

Because food rich in vitamins was so scarce, Opa and I scoured abandoned courtyards and mounds of rubble in search of nettles, edible roots or dandelion leaves, which we ate in salads. We had acquired oil to dress them with on the black market, in exchange for a Chinese porcelain tea service; Hilde would never willingly have parted with it, but it was too late now.

Our stepmother went regularly to Friedrichsruher Strasse to sort out the bomb-damaged flat. One day, she found news that my father had recovered, and that he would soon be granted leave. I saw that she was happy about this. I was happy too: at long last I would be able to hug my father again, and all my problems with my stepmother would be over. He would be bound to take my side! But there was bad news as well: Aunt Margarete had killed herself. Eva was staying with relatives pending my father's return.

One morning Opa asked us if we wanted to go on a little outing with him. Peter made a bit of a fuss: he preferred to stay at home and played dominoes with Hilde. But I was keen.

'Where are we going?' I asked, once we were outside.

'To find my glazier.'

'To put new windows in?'

'Well guessed!' he beamed.

Lothar Bucher Strasse was half-deserted. There was only a small group of women chatting by the advertising pillar. As we passed by them, I heard one of them exclaim, 'Not that story again, Friede! You would think you were the only woman ever to have been raped by the Russians! What would my cousin say to that? She was raped three times, *and* got pregnant!'

The road was still pitted with craters; whole blocks of flats had been reduced to piles of rubble. Fortunately the corpses had been taken away, along with the wreckage that had piled up by the footpaths.

In the gardens of bombed-out houses, birds sang their hearts out and roses blossomed; jasmine bushes filled the air with their intoxicating scent. It was a beautiful day. A turquoise arc stretched peacefully over the city, as though to bring consolation to the great sea of destruction.

Various vehicles passed by, driven by Russians. The first few paid no attention to us, but then one of them stopped, and a Russian leapt out, shouting, '*Stoj! Dokumenty!*' A very young man with a freckled face, he smelled of bread. Carefully checking our papers, he asked Opa, nodding towards me, 'The . . . child . . . how you say *dochka*?' Then a hint of embarrassment flitted across his face. '*Nyet*,' he corrected himself, 'the child . . . how you say?'

'Granddaughter,' said Opa.

'*Da*, granddaughter!'

'Yes, she's my granddaughter,' Opa confirmed.

The Russian nodded, winked at me, handed the papers back to Opa, said, '*Do svidaniya* granddaughter' and waved us on our way.

'Why are they still checking papers?' I asked.

'They're in charge now,' Opa explained.

'Are they going to stay here forever?'

'They'll go sooner or later.'

'When?'

'Maybe in a few years.'

'Years!'

'They can occupy our country for as long as they like,' Opa replied. But when I asked if we were going to become Russian, he gave a sly smile. 'A German can never become a Russian, my child!' I couldn't tell if that was meant as a compliment to the Russians or the Germans.

'So who's worse, the Russians or the Germans?' I asked. He replied benignly, 'Every nation has its good people and its bad people; perhaps there is a tendency in the German nation that seems less pronounced among the Russians. You might call it fanaticism.'

'What is fanaticism?'

'Fanaticism is when you do things with such exaggerated commitment that you become blind and deaf and uncritical.'

'What's uncritical?'

'That's when you give up judging, interpreting or evaluating the results of your work or your activities, or even other people's attitudes. For example, the German people, or many of them, maintained an uncritical position towards Hitler, officially at least.'

'The headmistress of my boarding school said the Führer was a bad man,' I remarked. 'She said he was a racist.'

'She was critical,' Opa replied, 'and brave as well.'

'Why?'

'Because Nazism was a repressive regime, so it was forbidden to criticise it.'

'What does that mean?'

'It was forbidden not to agree with the Führer's ideas.'

'Is that why they burned the books of writers who said bad things about Nazism?'

'That's right. Who told you that?'

'The headmistress.'

Opa was about to add something, but all of a sudden he muttered, 'And this is where he lived!' We had stopped in front of a heavily bombed building. Half of the front door hung drunkenly from its hinges. The place was silent and utterly forlorn. Long yellow grass sprouted from among the slabs of the short path leading up to the door; on it lay the marble bust of a Nazi hero, upon whose decorated chest a witty bird had built its nest. There was no trace of a human presence.

The courtyard was submerged in exuberant vegetation, the May wind bent the tips of the unmown grass that covered everything; an iron bench peeped out from a forest of weeds. The birds sang wildly, and lizards sped over the sunlit remains of walls. There was a kind of ambiguous enchantment in the air: spring had prevailed.

The place bewitched me, and I plonked myself down on the grass. Opa had a rest on the bench; I could only see the parting of his hair. I called to him, and he answered, but we couldn't see one another, and I thought that was funny. I looked at the sky and heard the bees. I inhaled the fresh smell of the grass and remembered Eden. How I longed to see the headmistress and Dr Löbig again!

Then Opa got up from the bench and, gazing around him like a sailor studying the horizon, saw the cabin. 'Shall we go and see who's in there?' he called.

'Who?'

'The glazier!' He started parting the sea of grass, and when he reached the cabin, he and his glazier hugged one another emotionally. 'You're alive, my lawyer friend, what joy!' sobbed the old craftsman, dabbing away his tears with the corner of his worn overalls. They started telling their stories: Opa talked about our cellar, the glazier about his. Opa about our sufferings, the glazier about his. Opa about our building, which had miraculously remained standing, and the glazier about his, which had collapsed like a house of cards.

The glazier's workshop had been in the basement of his block, and when he had thought he was done for, between one air-raid warning and another, he had started to drag big sheets of glass to the cabin, storing them between thick layers of glass fibre. 'That's how they survived the bombs,' the man said radiantly. 'The Ivans knocked the building down, but they couldn't smash my glass!' He rubbed his hands together as though he had played a clever trick on someone.

'So can you replace the windows in my daughter's flat?' Opa asked hopefully.

The glazier promised to do the job as soon as he could find petrol for his old van, which was parked under a clump of whispering birch trees. 'Of course I'll have to ask the authorities for permission to start working again,' he added, 'but that shouldn't be a problem: there are no windows anywhere in the city!' And he rubbed his hands again. He looked as pleased as punch.

Finally the glazier showed us the precarious dwelling he had made for himself in a corner of the cabin: a camp bed, a dented chair, some wooden chests that served as wardrobes, a three-legged table propped up by boxes. A widower since the first days of the war, the man looked like a sailor who had survived a shipwreck.

Opa and the glazier said their farewells and off we went again. I in my little cotton dress, rather American in style (my stepmother had swapped Opa's telescope for it on the black market), and Opa in his perfectly pressed dark grey suit. We felt like aristocrats; in a few days we might even have glass in our windows!

Further along, on a shutter, someone had crossed out the word *JUDE* and written underneath it, in blood-red paint, *HITLER MURDERER*.

XIX

Berlin, July 1945

The glazier replaced the window-panes in Hilde's flat.
Looking through them, we could see the ruins
opposite in all their mute bewilderment; there was
also a clear view of the advertising pillar, carrying
General Berzarin's reassurance regarding the Soviet
administration's intentions. And, beneath the
ordinances, the first timid posters advertising events
in the theatres or concert halls that were reopening
their doors.

It was down to the women that the streets were now
free of rubble, though armies of rats continued to
multiply undisturbed. On the main thoroughfares we
were starting to hear the ringing of the tram bells
again, and the *U-Bahn* and elevated railways were
being repaired, one length of track at a time. Progress
was being made with rationing, but we were still
hungry. There was no milk for children, and many of
us suffered from vitamin deficiencies.

Hilde had recovered almost completely and took
long walks in the area around Lothar Bucher Strasse.
Each time she came back, she expressed her

astonishment at the extent of the destruction, and each time she discovered another shattered landmark – the building housing her hairdresser, the pharmacy or the baker on the corner of Bismarckstrasse. Opa had started small-scale inquiries about friends and relatives, and the results were shocking. The authorities were unable to supply reliable information, because the census of survivors was still under way.

Sometimes I heard talk of atrocious crimes that were supposed to have been committed in the Nazis' concentration camps, but they were mentioned in the hushed, cautious tones you use when you have difficulty believing news that shakes your conscience to the core. I remembered the things the two mothers had said in the Chancellery bunker, finally understanding their meaning; so was it true that the Nazis had killed all those Jews? I thought about Herr Schacht, dragged away so brutally by the Gestapo, and of the sister of the headmistress at Eden, deported to a camp along with her twins. One day I tried to talk to Opa about it, but I found him strangely reluctant; perhaps he didn't want to upset me. I tried again with Hilde, but she asked me crisply to avoid the subject in future, dismissing me with the words 'Let posterity judge.'

One morning Opa, Peter and I went with our stepmother to the flat in Friedrichsruher Strasse. It was a beautiful day, and the shrill cries of children rang out from Lauenburger Platz. Bismarckstrasse was very busy, the footpaths were crowded with people, and the bells of the trams jangled.

The building looked different to me, not as tall as I remembered, and the façade was riddled with bullet-holes. On the path, lined with perfectly trimmed box hedges, there was a big crater that had not yet been filled in; the double door hung from its hinges. The concierge, a new one (her predecessor had been killed while fetching water), complained that at night anyone at all could come into the hallway and steal things from those flats that were still empty, like our own. Other tenants, in fact, were still unaccounted for; there had been no news, for example, of a mother with two little children who had regularly taken refuge in an air-raid shelter near Thorwaldsenstrasse.

The flat was already in a good state of repair. Ursula had managed to get the front door back on its hinges, and Opa's glazier had replaced the broken window-panes. The concrete balcony looked out over Bismarckstrasse and a sea of ruins. Soon my father would be back, and we would start living as a proper family again. Would it work? I was worried, and I also wondered whether I would still be able to see Opa whenever I wished to.

'I want to see my room!' Peter shouted.

'You're going to be sharing with your sister,' our stepmother said.

'I want my own room!' Peter demanded.

'I repeat, you're going to be sharing with your sister,' Ursula replied patiently.

'What happened to that seventeenth-century table?' Opa asked, to change the subject.

'The bookshelf fell on it,' our stepmother replied. 'I found it in bits.'

'I want my room!' bleated Peter.

'Shame,' commented Opa, 'it was quite unique, I'll never find another one like it.'

Peter tugged at Ursula's skirt. 'Why can't Helga sleep in the drawing room?'

'I don't think that's a good idea, my love,' said our stepmother, and Peter exploded into a rage. Opa said to his daughter, 'That boy is spoilt,' but she laughed. 'No, he's just got character. He's a true German!'

The day of my father's return duly arrived, and we all assembled in Friedrichsruher Strasse to welcome him. For the umpteenth time Peter asked, 'Who's coming on the train? And what's his name?'

'His name's Stefan and he's your father,' our stepmother replied, 'and stop asking me.'

'Why has Stefan never come to see us?' Peter insisted.

'You're to call him Papa, not Stefan.'

'Stefan sounds nicer.'

'Papa!'

'Why has Stefan never come to see us?' Peter urged.

Ursula sighed. 'Because he was at the front, and you're to call him Papa!'

'I'm shy.'

'But he's your father!'

'I'm shy.'

Our stepmother rose from the sofa. 'That's enough nonsense out of you, young man. I'm going to get ready.'

'I'm going to the station too!'

'No!' said Ursula, adding, 'He's my husband, darling!'

'Mine too! Mine too!'

'God almighty, he's your father, Peter!'

Peter stuck out his tongue and she thumbed her nose at him. Sometimes I envied Peter his confidence with her.

When she reappeared she looked terribly pretty. She was wearing a light-coloured suit with shoulder-pads and a narrow waist, sheer stockings that had cost her a silver candelabra on the black market, and a little pillbox hat. After she left, Opa, Peter and I went for a walk to pass the time. Hilde stayed at home reading a book.

Once he was outside, Peter wanted to climb into the crater in the path to play war, and we had a consider-able amount of trouble getting him back out of it. Finally he walked ahead of us skipping and chanting 'My father's coming today! My father's coming today!'

Past the crossroads we saw some children playing among the ruins. Peter stopped and called bossily 'Hey, you lot!'

They all turned around, and a little girl replied irritably, 'What do you want?'

'What's that game you're playing?' asked Peter, his fists on his hips; he was becoming as cheeky as he had been before.

The little girl tilted her head, tried to smile, failed and replied gruffly, 'Mummies and daddies.'

'My father's coming this evening!' Peter announced importantly.

The little girl twisted the hem of her pinafore and replied, 'My father's in Heaven over Russia.'

'Where?'

'Maybe she means that her father was killed in Russia,' suggested Opa.

'My father wasn't killed,' Peter announced coarsely, 'and this evening he's coming on the train.'

The little girl shrugged and turned towards her companions, but Peter shouted at her back, 'Have you at least got a grandfather?'

She turned to look at him, and her face was twisted and resentful; finally she attempted another smile. Slipping her hand into the pocket of her pinafore, she asked, 'Do you want a sweet?'

Peter went over to her and took something out of her hand, but before he could put it in his mouth Opa stopped him: 'Show me what it is!'

'No!'

'Show me.' It was a throat pastille. 'That isn't a sweet,' said Opa. 'Throw it away!'

'No!'

'It's good,' the girl shouted. 'We have loads of them at home, my dad was a doctor!'

'Throw it away, Peter!'

But my disobedient little brother threw the pastille into his mouth. It went down the wrong way; he started coughing and went purple in the face. Opa slapped him on the back. Once the crisis was over, Opa said, 'Let's go home now.'

Time wouldn't pass.

Finally we heard my stepmother's key in the lock: they were back! My heart leapt into my throat. We all dashed into the corridor. I saw a tall, thin man in a uniform. He had black, wavy hair, a bit grizzled at the temples, and he was smiling. Standing out in his gaunt face were two black eyes which I did not recognise; I don't know why, but I had imagined my father's eyes were blue! I was seized with such violent emotion that I had to run to the toilet.

Joining everyone in the drawing room, I found Peter sitting on our father's lap, crowing, '. . . and then I said "I'm fine, Herr Hitler, what a lovely buckle, Herr Hitler!"' He peered at Papa to see his reaction. But my father put Peter down on the floor and came over to me. In disappointment Peter yelled, 'Stefan is mine, he's my Stefan!' and stamped his feet.

Murmuring, 'How are you, my child?' my father hugged me. I couldn't reply. Feeling that I was safe at last, I wept in my father's arms.

XX

Berlin, August 1945

I had placed great hopes on my father's return, certain that I would find an ally in him: soon he was bound to notice the coldness with which my stepmother treated me and persuade her to change her attitude. But from the very first my father revealed himself to be an introverted man, and I felt him becoming more remote by the day. He was awkward with Peter and me, as though he had lost the habit of being a father. When Peter sulked or snapped bossily as he often did, my father merely glanced at Ursula with faint bewilderment, leaving her with the task of correcting his son, which she did not always do. I felt that my father was passive, that he was not playing his part.

He also spent many hours in his study, reading, writing and sometimes painting. I was disappointed. In my father's presence my stepmother treated me with unfamiliar indulgence, behaving in the maternal way she usually reserved for Peter. My brother thought he noticed a threat to his own privileged position and reacted with violent fits of jealousy.

I felt confused and unhappy.

When our stepmother went to the food-distribution office to claim her rations, she would usually leave Peter with me. The minute she left home, my father would withdraw to his study, staying there until she came back. It was as though he was avoiding finding himself face to face with his children, and that annoyed me. So I decided to win him over.

One day when Ursula was out, I burst into his study with such force that I nearly crashed into his desk. My father, who had been writing a letter, looked at me with calm disappointment: 'Is this how you come into a room?' I blushed violently and shook my head. He looked at me for a long time, then said, 'In future, remember to knock before entering.' I nodded, then there was a long silence. 'Was there anything you wanted to tell me?' he asked finally, his eyes fixed once more on his letter. I nodded again but felt stiff and embarrassed; my heart was overflowing with things I wanted to say, and I couldn't get a single word out. So I gave up, apologised and left the room.

Some days later I resumed the attack. One morning – Ursula had just closed the door behind her – I knocked at the study door. 'Come in!' said my father. I went in hopefully. However, before I could open my mouth, he stopped me: 'I have to finish an urgent letter, Helga, would you mind coming back in ten minutes?'

I went back to the kitchen, where Peter was busy unscrewing the knobs from the kitchen drawers. He was always yielding to destructive impulses, and to add insult to injury he always tried to blame me for the damage. I yelled at him, and as I tried to put the knobs back on, Peter challenged me: 'I was going to say that you did it!' I was tempted to slap him, but I held myself back. He would have howled the place down, and my father would have been worried. So I invented a game to distract him, and fortunately he played it enthusiastically, not least because I always let him win.

About ten minutes later I knocked at the study door again, but my father still hadn't finished. 'Sorry, I'll be another quarter of an hour, I'll call you.' I went back to the kitchen, where Peter had started unscrewing the knobs once more. I got so annoyed that I developed a terrible headache. I put the knobs back on while Peter tickled me. About a quarter of an hour passed, but by the time my father called me I could hear the front door opening: Ursula was back. So of course that was the end of it.

Peter took a sudden interest in our father as well. At first he had felt uneasy with him, but now he was curious. He was always around Papa, demanding his attention. He followed him everywhere, even waiting for him outside the bathroom door! My father soon grew annoyed, or perhaps he was frightened. But Peter insisted. He was forever bursting into the study without knocking, he wanted to be with his Papa. He badgered him with questions and demanded exhaustive answers. Eventually my father was seized by something like panic, and for two days he locked himself in his study. But Peter was neither patient nor diplomatic, and he was also used to winning people over from the very first, without having to employ all his forces. He persisted, and my father beat a retreat. But the more he sought refuge from his son, the more persistently Peter followed him! I don't know what impulse drove my brother; perhaps he wanted to recover a figure whose symbolic role had for a time been filled by Hitler. But our father did not yield to his son's violence, and their relationship, rather than becoming more solid, was stretched to breaking point. Disappointed and shaken by this rejection, Peter intensified his attachment to our stepmother.

Early one morning my father took his easel, his stool and his box of colours to go and paint outdoors. Exhilarated by the prospect, I asked to go with him, but he refused. I insisted. I saw the outing as an opportunity to get closer to this man, to build a bridge between us. But he didn't want me to go. He tried various excuses, telling me, for example, that I was bound to get bored. I wouldn't give in.

'I prefer to be alone when I'm painting,' he replied uneasily.

'Please!'

He looked at me, his face undecided and slightly annoyed. How distant he seemed at that moment! In the end he changed his mind and agreed, the way one does when giving in to the entreaties of an inveterate nuisance. 'All right then, come on!' So we set off together.

We walked among ruins and flattened squares, finally taking the elevated railway. The train was half-empty, and it had glass in its windows. We passed by scenes consisting entirely of rubble, piles of stones and dusty wreckage. After two stops we got out.

We walked along a wide, tree-lined avenue: here too there were ruins and more ruins. Rays of sunlight passed between the blackened walls, gilding the grim mounds as though to provide a little comfort.

My father had not spoken a word on the journey, and he continued to say nothing, responding to my shy approaches with the briefest of grunts. Finally I gave up speaking.

After a crossroads, we turned into a little path leading to what must once have been a kind of villa. The ruins lay deep within an overgrown and abandoned garden, an explosion of roses among the rampant grass.

My father had stopped and was contemplating the ruined building. Then he said, taking me by surprise, 'My brother-in-law gave this villa to my sister when she turned twenty-five. They seemed so happy . . .' I didn't dare to comment. He had already set off towards the pile of rubble; climbing up on to it, he set up his easel. He placed his paints within reach, unfolded his stool, slipped his palette over his thumb and began to paint.

I watched him sketch out the first few marks and immediately realised that he had no intention of painting the ruin or the blossoming garden, but only the flowers that grew in the debris. There were flowers of many kinds, pale and delicate, humble, rubble-grown flowers. My father painted for almost two hours without interruption, forgetting I was there. Because I didn't want to disturb him, I tried to find something to distract me. So I started searching among the wreckage and found some interesting things: a doll's head with eyes that moved, a coffee-pot without a spout and a white telephone receiver. I hurried over to my father to show him my treasures, but he merely murmured, 'How lovely . . .' without raising his eyes from the canvas. Then, just to provoke a reaction, I said, 'The villa in Tempelhof is prettier!'

He stopped painting and, as though reassembling a jigsaw puzzle I had disarranged, replied, 'But she was happy here!' Then he went back to work. I realised there was no point trying any further, climbed down from the rubble and went to sleep under a tree. I awoke at the sound of my father's voice calling to me. The sky was clouding over. The air was still, there was not so much as a breath of wind. An army of ants was marching over my arm, and I brushed them away. I went over to my father.

The painting was finished. I studied it admiringly. There was all the splendid, spontaneous flora of the rubble: harebells, leopard's bane, little gentians, pinks and wild narcissi. It was a beautiful big painting, and I exclaimed, worried, 'You're not going to sell it!' In fact he never did, and my brother still has it.

'These days people want bread, not paintings,' my father replied darkly.

'Aren't you going to be a painter?' I asked, disappointed.

'No,' he replied curtly, and with the tip of his index finger he added one last nuance to the petal of a tiny periwinkle.

'Why not?' I insisted.

'It's not a good job anymore.'

'So what are you going to do?'

'We'll go back to Austria, and I'll find a job.'

'To Austria!' I exclaimed in surprise.

'We are Austrians,' he reminded me. 'I don't want to stay in this country, in this city. There is nothing for me here.'

'And . . . Ursula?' I asked cautiously.

'Ursula is my wife, and by marrying me she has the right to Austrian citizenship.'

'So we're going to leave Berlin?'

'I'll go on ahead.'

'When?'

'Soon. As soon as the authorities give me permission.'

'You're going to leave . . .' I murmured, broken-hearted.

'I'm going to have to find a job,' he repeated in a practical voice, 'and a house. We can't all just set off blindly.' I looked for a long time at that unknown father whom I loved but who didn't know how to talk to me properly, and I cried, shaking with rebellious fury, 'You can't leave me alone again!'

He looked at me in astonishment. 'But your mother will be there!'

'She's not my mother!' I exploded furiously.

'She's your new mother,' he replied, without losing his composure, 'and you've got to learn to accept her, Helga.'

'She doesn't love me!' I shrieked.

'But she does,' he replied calmly.

'That's not true!' I cried. 'She doesn't love me, and

she never has! That's why I hid in the cellar! That's why she sent me to that institution where they cut my hair off! That's why she sent me to Eden! She's always wanted to get rid of me, always, always!' I panted and watched him, hoping I had shifted something in his heart. But he replied, in a measured paternal voice, 'You needed looking after.'

'Dr Löbig said I only needed a mother!' I shouted, and burst into tears because I couldn't break down the wall that divided us. Drying my eyes, I added rancorously, 'Why didn't you leave us with Grandmother? She loved us!'

'Grandmother is old. How could she have brought up two little children?'

'I want my mother!' I declared.

His face darkened, and he looked at me with growing concern. The calm slipped from his face like an avalanche.

'I want my mother!' I repeated impulsively, excitedly, heedlessly. 'She loves me, I know she does! She's my mother! I want her! What did she do to you? Why didn't you want to see her anymore? Why did she go? She loves me, I know she does! She loves me!' I was beside myself.

My father had clenched his fists, and a vein stood out on his temple. His expression darkened, his face twitched, and I grew afraid. Finally he shouted in a voice that threatened to break, 'If your mother had loved you, she wouldn't have left you for the Führer!' He grabbed the canvas from the easel, threw the tubes of paint into the box without screwing on the caps, folded up his stool, picked everything up and said abruptly, 'Let's go!' He set off at such a pace that I had trouble keeping up with him. I trotted along like a whipped puppy, feeling guilty. I tried to ask his forgiveness, but he wouldn't listen. We ran to the *S-Bahn* station; I was breathless, and my legs were trembling. It was not until we were on the train that my father said to me, more calm and controlled now, 'No, *you* must forgive *me*. But stay off certain subjects in future. When you grow up you'll understand.'

It had been my last chance to establish some sort of rapport between my father and myself, and I had thrown it away.

XXI

I no longer had any doubt that my father was very much in love with our stepmother; so many things confirmed the fact. For example, I had discovered that he wrote her a love letter every day; she would tuck them under her pillow. They were all decorated with little flowers and pierced little hearts, and filled with sweet nothings; as I read them, I simmered with disdainful jealousy. He squandered his attention on his wife, while he was reserved and detached with us, his children. I couldn't figure it out. I was annoyed that I had discovered my father's passionate temperament before his paternal qualities, which remained entirely obscure to me.

After some time the authorities granted us permission to repatriate to Austria, and my father prepared to leave. We were to join him as soon as he managed to create a secure base for the four of us, but that could take many months. Austria had the same problems as Germany: unemployment, poverty and a housing shortage.

Because Ursula and my father had been apart for so long, they spent every available moment on their own, trying to get rid of Peter and me for a few hours. But

Opa was not well and could not look after us, so it was up to me to look after my brother whether I wanted to or not.

A swimming-pool had opened in our neighbourhood, and one day my stepmother suggested that we go there. Peter jumped for joy, and I was also enthusiastic. I had no idea what a swimming-pool was like, but I understood that it had something to do with water, an element I genuinely adored since it had been denied me for so long.

No sooner said than done! Ursula prepared us a little parcel of food to eat and gave me a list of things to remember when looking after Peter. Then she handed me two bathing costumes she had acquired on the black market and walked us to the tram stop. Peter was in seventh heaven and, when he saw the jangling tram coming, started jumping up and down and clapping his hands; he didn't even want to say goodbye to our stepmother, and dragged me towards the tram as though he had lost his mind.

The carriage was half-empty, and Peter sat on all the seats until he found one particularly to his liking. The seats were made of gleaming wood, and he rubbed the bottom of his shorts against them; he breathed on the window, drew a bomb with his finger and commented loudly on everything he saw passing by, while the other passengers glared at us with irritation. By the time we reached our stop, he didn't want to get out; he was so wild about travelling by tram that he was even prepared to give up the idea of the swimming-pool. I literally had to drag him from the carriage while he wriggled and kicked, casting me in a bad light as usual.

Fortunately he was spellbound as soon as we reached the pool entrance, which was right opposite the tram stop. We passed through a big front door with the word *FREIBAD* above it in big letters.

The ticket office was a concrete cube. Inside it sat a middle-aged woman who scowled at us severely: 'Can you swim, children?' Peter nodded automatically, while I told the truth: 'No.'

'Then you'd better not leave the children's pool!' snarled the woman, jabbing a cigarette between her lips and handing me the tickets and a cabin key.

The place was deserted, and I was overjoyed at the sight of the two pools: so much water! It was incredible; I thought I was dreaming.

It was a beautiful day, and the sun gleamed on the water; reflections trembled on the bottom. The children's pool was smaller than the one for adults. 'I'm going in that one,' Peter announced. 'It looks nicer.'

'You can't,' I told him.

'Why?'

'You're not allowed in there.'

'I'm not allowed?'

'The water goes higher than your head!'

'That doesn't matter.'

'If you don't know how to swim, you'll drown!'

'No!'

I dragged Peter towards the cabin, worried that he might start his usual performance. He often enjoyed pretending not to understand just to provoke me, but this time I wasn't in the mood to argue. I wanted to get into the water!

The cabin was a small wooden box with a little

sloping roof. There was a bench inside, and various hooks on the walls for hanging your clothes. We got undressed, put on our costumes and ran outside. Peter stopped at the edge of the adult pool, but the woman at the ticket office shouted, 'Get over to the children's pool this minute, you stupid boy!' Peter complied. But the moment my terrible little brother dipped his foot in the water he exclaimed, 'It's freezing!' and dashed back to the cabin. I called him several times, but he didn't reappear, so I forgot about him and entered the pool until I was up to my neck. The water turned out to be lukewarm. I felt very happy.

I plunged my head beneath the surface, opened my eyes and looked up; the water shivered as though swept by the wind. The sky looked wavy, the colour of night. I became frightened. When I surfaced, I saw it was calm and blue; I felt more at ease. Never again would I see skies as clear as the one over Berlin immediately after the war.

Finally I decided to get out, not least because my fingers were wrinkling. When I returned to the cabin I found Peter looking like the cat who had got the cream. It took only a glance to work out that he had eaten all our supplies, my ration included! I was absolutely furious. Being in the water had made me very hungry. I shouted, 'You never change! You're a thief!' and gave him a slap. He stood motionless, staring at me, his face filled with hatred. All of a sudden he dashed out of the cabin and threw up into the pool.

The woman in the ticket office came running and started bellowing at us. She called us gypsies, vandals, cockroaches, the kind of people who polluted public spaces. 'Get out!' she yelled, pointing towards the exit with a quivering finger. 'I don't want to see you anywhere near this place again, or I'll call the police.'

Of course she was exaggerating, but I was mortified. I pushed Peter into the cabin and forced him to get dressed. He didn't want to know about it. I very nearly gave him another slap. Dressed once more, we sped past the ticket office and made off. I was so furious that I didn't talk to Peter for the whole tram journey home. He breathed on the glass, maintaining a long face as he drew various different types of bomb with his finger. Once we got off the tram, I began to worry: we hadn't been at the pool for more than half an hour, so our stepmother would be angry with me.

Once we were home, I rang the doorbell for a long time. Our neighbour, now an elderly lady with a paraplegic daughter, poked her head out of her front door to ask if we had been locked out. At that very moment our stepmother opened the door, a strange expression on her face. She was wrapped in a shiny dressing gown I had never seen her wearing before and asked acidly, 'Back already? How lovely . . .' Then she shouted towards the matrimonial bedroom, 'Those rogues are back already, Stefan!' And she vanished into the bathroom.

She didn't want to know what had happened at the pool and told Peter to be quiet when he started telling one of his usual lies. She sent us to our room, and Peter, bewildered, dealt an angry kick to a bed-leg.

A few days later I was given an opportunity to

recover a little of Ursula's esteem. She sent me to collect a package of oil paints for my father. He was working on a portrait of her and wanted to finish it before he left for Austria. Of course I had to bring my terrible little brother with me.

The place was not far away, just a few tram stops.

This time our stepmother didn't give us any food to take with us, but she did let us have some money to buy ice cream. The first ice-cream parlours in the city were just opening, and people were crowding around them, attracted by the novelty. For Peter and me, ice cream was a completely unknown delicacy.

We got out at the fourth stop, as our stepmother had advised us to; then I had to ask a passer-by the way to the building whose street and number were written on a piece of paper. I stopped an old man, who said, 'At the end of the street, little one, you can't miss it, it's the only house still standing.' I also inquired about an ice-cream parlour, and he pointed towards it, saying, 'There, where the queue is.'

We joined the queue, and Peter immediately became impatient. Finally it was our turn, and we asked for two vanilla ice creams. As fate would have it, the ice cream was rather hard and wedged between two wafers; the minute we left the shop, Peter's ice cream slipped from the wafers and fell to the ground. He stood there holding the wafers, literally speechless. After a few moments he uttered a howl of protest so agonising that people rushed out of the shop to see what had happened. Peter was shrieking that he wanted my ice cream; it never occurred to me to let him have it. If he had lost his own, so much the worse for him! But Peter was howling and throwing himself on the ground, he wanted my ice cream at any cost. A lady came over to me and said threateningly, 'Just give him the ice cream!' I defended myself: 'He dropped his!' But the woman didn't believe me. 'That's quite enough nonsense, little girl, give your brother the ice cream! I take it that little angel is your brother, isn't he?' Two gimlet eyes pierced me. 'Yyyyes . . .' I muttered between my teeth.

'Then give him the ice cream!' the woman repeated in a tone so harsh that it frightened me. I gave up my ice cream with hatred in my heart.

Peter's face immediately lit up with satisfaction, and he started licking greedily, making my fingers itch. I hated him! I strode off furiously so that he would at least have difficulty keeping up with me and his haste would prevent him from enjoying his ice cream! He came panting after me, still licking away. But all of a sudden a piece of wafer went down the wrong way: he started coughing and spluttering, so I had to stop to help him. I slapped him on the back as Opa had done when he choked on the throat pastille, and after a while he recovered. His face was red and sweaty, his eyes wide, but he nonetheless swallowed the last scrap of wafer and licked his fingers. He then complained that his fingers were sticky. I told him to spit on them and clean them with some grass, which – improbably – he did.

We hurried along the tree-lined avenue, melancholy ruins on either side. The asphalt was still pitted with craters; Peter tried to hide in one of them. I didn't deign to comment, so he started sulking and I heard him muttering behind me: 'Helga's a silly goat! Helga's an idiot!' For a while I ignored him, but when I eventually turned around, I saw that he was picking up some berries that had fallen from the trees and was about to put them in his mouth. 'What on earth are you eating?' I yelled. 'Show me!' He obeyed, more because I was shouting so loudly than because of anything else. They were little red fruits, about the size of maize kernels. I tried a few: they were sweet and floury. If anyone was going to be poisoned, at least it would be me!

Peter watched me with great interest, asking me every now and again whether I was dying or not, because he was hungry. He was truly cynical. When it was clear that I hadn't died, we picked up a large quantity of the little red balls and filled our stomachs. Continuing on our way, we found the building we were looking for. There was a sign on the door – 'Waldpach – paints and colours' – and, beneath it, in smaller letters, 'In the cellar'.

We entered through the half-open door and found ourselves in a gloomy hall. A black arrow pointed us towards the cellar. We climbed down a badly lit staircase with loose steps. There was an inviting smell of food. At the foot of the stairs we saw the words 'Waldpach – at the end of the corridor'.

We passed two closed doors, but the third was open, and we saw to our astonishment that it led to a kitchen. That was where the smell of food was coming from! After a moment's hesitation, I went in with Peter, who was clinging to my clothes.

There was a smoking wood stove, a pot of potatoes

boiling away on top. Another pot had been removed from the fire and was full of meatballs. Real meatballs!

I stared at the delicious food and thought I might faint. Hunger gripped me so violently that, as though in a trance, I stretched out my hand, extracted a meatball from the sauce and slipped it into my mouth. I almost passed out with pleasure. The rest took only a moment: I filled all the pockets of my dress with meatballs, took Peter's hand, and we both made a run for it. When we reached the street, we went on running as though the Devil himself was in hot pursuit, until I had to stop because of the violent stitches in my side. Peter immediately started pestering me: 'I want some meatballs, I want them!' I gave him one, hoping that would satisfy him, but he protested: 'You have more, I want more too!' So I divided the booty into equal parts. He filled his trouser pockets with meatballs, and we ran on to the end of the avenue. Finally we stopped, sat down beneath a tree and ate all of them. It was only then that I realised how filthy we were, covered in grease from head to toe! Our stepmother would kill us! And I hadn't collected the package of paints!

When we got home, all Hell broke loose. Our stepmother beat us both with a leather strap and sent us to bed. The next day, even Papa gave us a severe talking-to. For a week an appalling atmosphere reigned in the house. I felt more uneasy than ever, not least because this time I really was in the wrong. Strangely, my father didn't go and collect the paints either, and the portrait of Ursula remained unfinished.

XXII

Berlin, end of June 1946

My father left as he had arrived, except that this time everything was topsy-turvy. We were in Lothar Bucher Strasse because Opa had had an attack of sciatica, and our stepmother was not euphoric but unhappy and downcast. My father said goodbye to Opa, telling him that he looked forward to a visit once Peter, Ursula and I had joined him, shook Hilde's hand, hugged Peter and me, and then he and Ursula set off for the station.

The minute they left, I was filled with a profound sense of abandonment. My father's stay had been like the passing of a shadow; now he was leaving Germany. Who could tell when I would see him again!

Peter was unmoved by his father's departure, having discovered that having him there and not having him there were one and the same. He wanted to drag me into Hilde's study, where he liked to bang away on the piano, but I refused. At the sight of my father's painting, I was sure I would burst into tears! So we went over to the drawing-room window to look down at the courtyard.

Everything was peaceful. The sun was shining, and the lime trees were covered with leaves.

The concierge had come out to sweep the path. Some children were playing ball, but I didn't know them: Egon wasn't there, and neither was Rudolf. Then I looked up towards the ruins surrounding the open space, and they made me feel strange. They no longer looked threatening; they had settled serenely into their surroundings, weird backdrops to a courtyard by now perfectly restored: the cracks in the paths had been filled with concrete, the rubble cleared away; the hedges had been trimmed, the grass cut. All trace of corpses purged. The shed repaired. There was a sense of order and normality. Further off, two women were beating carpets. Could they be Frau Bittner and Frau Mannheim? On a bench that had recently been returned to its place at the foot of the luxuriant lilac bush, an old man was enjoying the sun. Herr Hammer, perhaps? The ruins now seemed reconciled to the past, forgiving it too easily. I said something about this to Peter, but he put a finger his forehead and said, 'You're stupid.'

Perhaps he was right.

Having recovered from his sciatica, Opa visited us in Friedrichsruher Strasse every now and again. Sometimes he suggested going for a walk, but Peter usually refused. In that case I would go on my own with Opa. I was happier that way. There were always complications when Peter was around!

One day Opa took me to Lichtenberg cemetery, where his wife was buried. We left a bunch of wild flowers on the tombstone, which was close to the graves of Karl and Wilhelm Liebknecht, smashed by the Nazis like others belonging to people held to be enemies of the Reich simply for having different political ideas.

XXIII

Autumn 1946

I still felt uneasy with my stepmother. Fortunately school resumed and took me away from home for hours at a time.

I was in the third year of high school (I should have been in the fourth, but between 1944 and 1945 I had missed a year), and I liked it.

Peter was enrolled in the first year, and he gave himself such airs about it that it damaged my health for a week.

By now things were better organised, despite the fact that in 1945 it had become apparent that there was a severe shortage of teachers, because those who had been Nazis had been expelled from the profession. Textbooks from the Nazi period had also been banned, and because there were no new ones as yet we had to do without. Lessons concentrated on material which didn't have to be de-Nazified, so we talked a lot about Goethe and Schiller. One day a boy, trying to be funny, raised his arm and shouted, *'Heil Hitler!'* He was immediately suspended for a fortnight.

We were still starving, and everything was very complicated in the former capital of the Reich. The shops were short of goods, anything that could be found was expensive, and the *Deutschmark* was worthless. Hilde complained because she couldn't buy anything on her wages. Christmas 1946 was sad and impoverished; no presents, no tree.

Ursula was desperate because my father still hadn't found a proper job and was surviving by working as a day labourer for a local peasant in exchange for basic food and lodgings consisting of a little makeshift bedroom above a stable. There was a permanent cold war between her and me, and I only relaxed when I was at school or with Opa.

Towards the end of 1946 my father wrote to say that he had finally found a job, and that he had been reunited with his parents. My paternal grandparents, once my grandfather had also returned from the war, had rented a two-storey house on the Attersee in Upper Austria. We would be able to live on the first floor. I would finally see my grandfather and grandmother again, and above all my father! But my joy was tinged with sorrow: I would have to leave Opa, perhaps forever. In all likelihood I would never again see that good old man, so sensitive and humane, the only person ever to have shown me a little warmth.

The rest happened very quickly. Ursula cancelled her lease on the flat in Friedrichsruher Strasse, paying the arrears with the precious Persian carpet she had brought as her dowry; everything was sold because we were only able to leave the country with the contents of a single suitcase. Peter and I were taken out of school, and in the blink of an eye it was time for us to go. I was stunned and incredulous to be leaving Opa and Berlin.

XXIV

Berlin, spring 1947

Gatow military airport extends a noisy welcome. There are men in uniform everywhere. The runways are drenched in sunlight.

Peter presses Teddy to his chest, shrieking questions our stepmother doesn't answer. Finally he is spellbound by the metal gleam of the fighter-bomber on which we are about to leave Berlin. Ursula is downcast: saying goodbye to Hilde and Opa was extremely difficult.

At the bottom of the steps, an English soldier goes through the formalities. As he checks our documents, Peter peers keenly at the man's beret, which doesn't look like the Führer's. The soldier turns to Peter: 'What's the bear's name?' He speaks correct German with a slight English accent.

Peter blinks and stammers, 'Ttt . . . ttt . . .'

'What?'

'Teddy.'

'Does Teddy have a ticket?' the soldier asks in a professional voice.

Peter looks first stunned, then alarmed. 'No!'

'Then Teddy can't fly,' the soldier decrees.

Peter stares at the soldier with bewildered eyes and bursts into desperate tears. A smile spreads across the soldier's face. 'I was only joking, little boy; I'll make up for it straight away.' He hands Peter a signed and stamped document bearing the words 'Teddy has permission to fly.' My brother still has it.

Peter sighs with relief and smiles at the soldier as a tear like a drop of crystal slides slowly down his cheek. We are finally ready to embark.

The plane is a survivor of the recent war, and instead of regular seats we find rudimentary folding ones. There are ten passengers, six adults and four children. Peter goes and sits by the first window, breathes on the glass and draws a bomb with his finger.

No sooner have we sat down than a fanatical old man starts talking at length about the plane's technical specificiations, listing the bombs, mortars, cannon and whatever else it could have carried, and excitedly pointing to the place where the artillery would have been stored. But just as he is saying 'The muzzle velocity was synchronised with . . .' a woman leaps to her feet and cries in exasperation, 'Shut your mouth, for God's sake! The war is over!'

The man gives a start, hunches his shoulders and turns his face towards the window.

Peter is agitated. He is forever jumping up, peering out on one side, then on the other, making little sounds of astonishment, of nervous expectancy. Finally a flight attendant, a young woman wearing a uniform and a beret, pulls him into line – 'It's time for you to calm down, young man' – and fastens his seat-belt. She fastens the other passengers' seat-belts as well, and shortly afterwards the loudspeaker informs us that the plane is about to take off. I concentrate on the window, too. There is a sharp smell of petrol.

Then the powerful engines roar. At the very last moment a little boy starts protesting: 'I want to get out! I'm scared!' But the noise drowns his voice.

The plane sets off down the glittering runway before rumbling into the air. The control tower gets further away, grows smaller, becomes a vague dot. Goodbye, Berlin!

A lump rises in my throat, turns into a mountain, I can't breathe. I'm starting to panic. I'm about to leave Berlin.

I start to cry.

Why am I crying? I'm not leaving anything but my good old Opa. But how it hurts!

I'm leaving a city that has refused me everything: a mother, a father, my grandmother. A normal life, a tranquil childhood. A city that has given me only pain, deprivation, terror, worry, sadness, anxiety and despair. Why am I crying?

The vast field of ruins slips by beneath our eyes: buildings, churches, bridges, squares, a heritage reduced to crumbs.

The shimmering of the flames, the smell of burning. The stench of the corpses.

Ashes on the skin, *JUDE* on the shutters, the child beneath the lilac bush. The apple-sized bloodstain on the mattress, Gudrun's staring eyes, Erika's tureen. You *urri*? *Spasibo*.

And bombs and fire. Fire and destruction. Destruction of things, bodies, laws, traditions, the achievements of civilisation. Back to zero. The destruction of the very last brick, the very last tiny grain of hope.

Beneath the enamel blue of an indifferent sky the sea of ruins disappears into the distance, becomes a shapeless mass, but something down there is calling to me.

Because down there, among the grim remains of that vast extinguished bonfire, among the cracks in the tarmac, in the damp cellar in Lothar Bucher Strasse, among the kindly folds of Opa's crumpled coat, that is where my roots remain. Stupid, stubborn roots clinging to the place where my heart beat most desperately.

Goodbye, Berlin! The lump in my chest swells, suffocating me. Berlin is disappearing on the horizon, sinking into a veil of mist. I feel a chill breeze, a sense of emptiness. The engines roar, I focus my eyes: I can see nothing now.

Soon we will land in Lübeck, where a refugee camp will take us in. Perhaps hunger awaits until a goods train takes us to Austria.